Grief Diaries

How to Help the Newly Bereaved

A grief etiquette guide for how
to support someone facing loss

LYNDA CHELDELIN FELL
with
ERICA GALE BELTZ
ANNAH ELIZABETH
MARY LEE ROBINSON

FOREWORD BY THOMAS JACK BARNETTE
Award-winning educator and entrepreneur
Founder, American International Television

INTRODUCTION BY ANNAH ELIZABETH
Author & Founder of The Five Facets of Healing

Grief Diaries
How to Help the Newly Bereaved – 1st ed.
Lynda Cheldelin Fell/Erica Gale Beltz/Annah Elizabeth/Mary Lee Robinson
Grief Diaries www.GriefDiaries.com

Cover Design by AlyBlue Media, LLC
Interior Design by AlyBlue Media LLC
Published by AlyBlue Media, LLC

ISBN: 978-1-944328-09-2
Library of Congress Control Number: 2015916907
AlyBlue Media, LLC
Ferndale, WA 98248
www.AlyBlueMedia.com

This book is designed to provide informative narrations to readers. It is sold with the understanding that the writers, authors or publisher is not engaged to render any type of psychological, legal, or any other kind of professional advice. The content is the sole expression and opinion of the authors and writers. No warranties or guarantees are expressed or implied by the choice to include any of the content in this book. Neither the publisher nor the author or writers shall be liable for any physical, psychological, emotional, financial, or commercial damages including but not limited to special, incidental, consequential or other damages. Our views and rights are the same: You are responsible for your own choices, actions and results.

PRINTED IN THE UNITED STATES OF AMERICA

GRIEF DIARIES

TESTIMONIALS

"CRITICALLY IMPORTANT . . . I want to say to Lynda that what you are doing is so critically important." –DR. BERNICE A. KING, Daughter of Dr. Martin Luther King

"INSPIRATIONAL . . . Grief Diaries is the result of heartfelt testimonials from a dedicated and loving group of people. By sharing their stories, the reader will find inspiration and a renewed sense of comfort as they move through their own journey." -CANDACE LIGHTNER, Founder of Mothers Against Drunk Driving

"DEEPLY INTIMATE . . . Grief Diaries is a deeply intimate, authentic collection of narratives that speak to the powerful, often ambiguous, and wide spectrum of emotions that arise from loss." -DR. ERICA GOLDBLATT HYATT, Chair of Psychology, Bryn Athyn College

"HOPE . . . These stories reflect the authentic voices of individuals at the unexpected moment their lives were shattered and altered forever. Moments of strength in the midst of indescribable pain, resilience in the midst of rage; hope while mired in despair." —SHERIFF SADIE DARNELL, Chair, Florida Cold Case Advisory Commission

"ACCURATE . . . These accounts portray an accurate picture of just what full-force repercussions follow the taking of a life." JAY HOWELL, U.S. Senate Investigator and Cofounder—National Center for Missing & Exploited Children

"BRAVE . . . The brave individuals who share their truth in this book do it for the benefit of all." CAROLYN COSTIN, Founder—Monte Nido Treatment Centers

"VITAL . . . Grief Diaries gives voice to the thousands who face this painful journey every day. Often alone in their time of need, these stories will play a vital role in surrounding each reader with warmth and comfort as they seek understanding and healing in the aftermath of their own loss." -JENNIFER CLARKE, R.N., Perinatal Bereavement Committee at AMITA Health Adventist Medical Center

"HOPE AND HEALING . . . You are a pioneer in this field and you are breaking the trail for others to find hope and healing." -KRISTI SMITH, Bestselling Author & International Speaker

"A FORCE . . .The writers of this project, the Grief Diaries anthology series, are a force to be reckoned with. I'm betting we will be agents of great change." -MARY LEE ROBINSON, Author and Founder of Set an Extra Plate initiative

"MOVING . . . In Grief Diaries, the stories are not only moving but often provide a rich background for any mourner to find a gem of insight that can be used in coping with loss. Reread each story with pen in hand and you will find many that are just right for you." -DR. LOUIS LAGRAND, Author of Healing Grief, Finding Peace

"HEALING . . . Grief Diaries gives voice to a grief so private, most women bear it alone. These diaries can heal hearts and begin to build community and acceptance to speak the unspeakable. Share this book with your sisters, mothers, grandmothers and friends who have faced grief. Pour a cup of tea together and know that you are no longer alone." -DIANNA VAGIANOS ARMENTROUT, Poetry Therapist & Author of Walking the Labyrinth of My Heart: A Journey of Pregnancy, Grief and Infant Death

"STUNNING . . . Delving into the deepest recesses of the heartbroken, the reader easily identifies with the diverse collection of stories and richly colored threads of profound love that create a stunning read full of comfort and hope." -DR. GLORIA HORSLEY, President, Open to Hope Foundation

"WONDERFUL . . .Grief Diaries is a wonderful computation of stories written by the best of experts, the bereaved themselves. Thank you for building awareness about a topic so near and dear to my heart." -DR. HEIDI HORSLEY, Adjunct Professor, School of Social Work, Columbia University, Author, Co-Founder of Open to Hope Organization

How to Help the Newly Bereaved

DEDICATION

This book is dedicated to all
who share the journey.

CONTENTS

BY THOMAS JACK BARNETTE

FOREWORD

Sometimes a totally unexpected tragedy befalls you, like the loss of a loved one. My own tragedy happened one beautiful day while enjoying a vacation at Hilton Head Island in South Carolina. My thirty-eight year old wife, Helen, had lupus, a complicated and unpredictable disease. But she was feeling great so we went for a jog in the island sun. Helen then returned to our hotel room alone while our son, Billy, and I went to play a round of golf. Later, when our son and I returned to the hotel, we discovered Helen had been taken to the hospital.

Earlier, during our jog, Helen ignored the sun's ultraviolet rays which can adversely affect those with lupus. She had also read a national article about how high doses of aspirin can alleviate some of the symptoms of lupus. Unbeknownst to us, Helen tried it and it triggered a thinning of the blood. She began bleeding throughout her body. My beautiful wife and soul mate was in critical condition. I sat at her side, holding her ice-cold hand. Later that night, Helen passed away.

I was stunned. I couldn't talk or even cry. My emotions were not accepting the reality of Helen's death. Our son couldn't, or wouldn't, cry outwardly, but inside he was falling apart. His grief was tremendous, and continues to this day. I didn't know how to help myself, let alone how to comfort our son.

Helen was my soulmate. She was cheerful, intelligent, friendly, high energy, entertaining, and extremely witty. And she was never boring. We were married for twelve years when she died. Even now a moment doesn't go by that I don't think of Helen, for she had a profound impact on my life.

As a child, I learned from science that all matter cannot be destroyed; it only changes forms. I took comfort from this and knew that Helen was still here. For years, even after I remarried, I always sensed Helen nearby. I would see a figure walk by a door in the house, stand in a room, or walk down the stairs, and I knew it was Helen. Even though she has been gone for thirty years, I still see her image from the corner of my eye, and then she's gone.

I had a business adversary drop me a note shortly after learning of Helen's death. "Jack, life must go on," he said. His note was simple yet revealed a sensitivity I had never known he had, and it gave me great strength. We became friends from that moment on. Another major support for me has been Christ, who not only helped me through that tragedy, but many more yet to come. I eventually married again, a marriage that lasted nearly twenty years and produced two lovely children who I adore. They and my other children have been my strength and support.

Grief is not something that you can just get over or shake off. However it does change forms and in time you learn to live with it. Friends, family, colleagues, medical professionals, counselors and clergy can truly help. By looking through the eyes of the bereaved, you will see how the initial aftermath and resulting milestones affect the entire family. This is why this book is so important. *How to Help the Newly Bereaved* is a powerful tool and will be your guide to learn how to offer the priceless gift of support to someone during the most difficult time in one's life.

THOMAS JACK BARNETTE
Award-winning educator and entrepreneur
Founder, American International Television

BY ANNAH ELIZABETH

INTRODUCTION

Dear friends and family of the bereaved,

Thank you for your courage and compassion to be a part of your loved one's grief journey. You are sharing an unimaginable pain. You, too, may be experiencing your own level of grief, and may feel just as lost about what to do next.

Helping someone who is grieving is often as stressful as going through grief ourselves. Too often we find ourselves in strange territory, trying to relate to a loss we haven't experienced, or we discover we have experienced something similar and we still don't know what to say or what to do. There are several reasons this confusion and anxiety exist. At the top of that list are two simple truths. The first is that we label complex outcomes with simple words like adultery, cancer, child loss, death, foreclosure, homicide and suicide. Second, each loss is different for every person, for we bring to the table different experiences, beliefs, abilities and values.

We say things like "I know how you feel, I've been there before," and "You are not alone." Sometimes those words bring comfort and sometimes they tip the rage scale. Why is that? "I've been there before," implies we know everything about what another is thinking, feeling and desiring. "You are not alone," is a cliché that slides off our tongues.

I like to say "We are neighbors in grief and allies in healing." Right next door are people who are experiencing various types of loss that we can relate to on some level, but the details are uniquely their own. The empathy and understanding is what makes us informed bystanders who might be able to provide some modicum of comfort. To that regard, we are never alone because there are millions of people who have experienced whichever one (or more) of those grief labels causing the pain.

Within these pages are suggestions and stories written by people who have traversed an assortment of tragedies. Though our stories, experiences and our expectations all vary, we have one thing in common: we all seek peace. Our hope is that within these pages you'll find nuggets of wisdom that help you better understand how to support someone in need.

Lastly, by reading this book because you want to help someone you love, then you already have the tools you need to help them, simply because you're reaching out. Follow your heart.

Yours in hope, healing and happiness,

ANNAH ELIZABETH
Founder, The Five Facets of Healing
www.annahelizabeth.com

CHAPTER ONE

WELCOME TO OUR WORLD

Love knows no difference
between life and death.

KHAN GHALIB

Neighbor Betty lost someone she loves and faces a long stretch of mourning. Now what? Should you mention her loved one? What if that makes her cry? Hesitant about choosing your words for fear you'll say something that makes the situation worse, you stumble through sentences and conversations become awkward. Let's face it, nothing you say can possibly make it any worse. Or can it?

While every loss is unique as a fingerprint, there is one thing we can say for sure: when Neighbor Betty finds herself on a journey through grief, she isn't there by choice. Truth be told, it's a foreign destination nobody wants to visit. There are no road signs, guide maps, or friendly hotels leaving the light on. Paralyzed with shock and sadness, Neighbor Betty has absolutely no idea which direction to go, or even how to start out on the journey. She would be ever so grateful for any support you offer.

Notice that we said *support*. Not *guidance*. We know you want to help, most people do. But how can you possibly guide Betty down the road if you aren't carrying her saddle? And grief is a saddle unlike any other, for no two losses are the same. While it's true that eventually the load lightens, the journey is much longer and more arduous than it looks. It's one of life's great mysteries to those who haven't yet walked the road.

In an age when technology is rapidly changing, you would think we would be better prepared. But we're not. For many, it remains uncomfortable to discuss death and loss, so they don't. People fear their own mortality, which leaves them ill equipped to help someone else. Until now.

How to Help the Newly Bereaved is an etiquette guidebook on just that — how to help the newly bereaved. Because every loss is unique as a fingerprint, this book is created using the perspectives of twenty-two individuals who have been down the long, hard road known as grief. Some are certified grief recovery specialists, others are educators and advocates. All have walked the road. Who better to tell you what to do, what to say, and what not to do and say than the bereaved themselves?

In addition to offering suggestions, we help you understand the journey. Why do we cry one minute and laugh the next? What brings us comfort? What do we fear? Sharing our stories will help you understand our perspectives, which will give you better insight. This is important because what fits for one person might not fit the next. The stories will help you understand why.

Finally, there are nuggets of wisdom so important we chose to begin the first chapter with them. Absorbing them in their entirety will not only help you to better understand our rollercoaster ride, they will save you a fair bit of angst in your efforts to support us. You'll find them listed under the Forget Me Nots on page five. What are forget me nots? Little nuggets of wisdom worth remembering, posted in a list format for easy reference.

So what exactly do you need to know, and why should you know it? One statement we commonly hear by the newly bereaved is "I didn't know." Translation: I didn't know it would be this painful. Or difficult. And how could you? Grief isn't something that can be taught in class. It is a language learned only by experience. There simply is no other way.

It is common for the bereaved to hear irritating statements such as "I know how you feel. My cat died last month." We roll our eyes as a silent groan escapes our lips. Yes, it hurts to lose a beloved pet. Just ask any pet lover. But each loss is unique, therefore not comparable. There are similar commonalities between losses, such as two mothers both losing a teenage daughter. But the similarities might end there, for each individual has a unique set of filters. Their religious beliefs, cultural differences, and diverse socioeconomic backgrounds are just the beginning. It's also true to say that grief, once experienced, transcends all differences. Confusing? Yes. But it's also simple. Once you've walked the road, you get it. Until then, you won't.

But not to worry because now you have this book. Not only is it chock full of important forget me nots, even more valuable is the understanding and insight gained by reading the unique journeys experienced by the writers. Simply put, no two grievers react the same. Which means that a helpful guidebook shouldn't be written from one perspective.

So when Neighbor Betty loses a loved one, consider this your etiquette guidebook on what to say, what to do and what not to forget. It's important to remember that each chapter offers guidelines only, for there is no right or wrong way to mourn. But next time someone you know loses someone they love, you'll understand a little better and be a bit more prepared to offer support along the way.

Welcome to our world.

DID YOU KNOW?
There are many types of grief.

Mask

Absent

Normal

Chronic

Delayed

Distorted

Inhibited

Traumatic

Collective

Prolonged

Cumulative

Abbreviated

Anticipatory

Complicated

Exaggerated

Disenfranchised

Forget Me Nots

1. **You can't fix grief.**
   It's natural to want to fix things that are broken, but grief is beyond your repair. Don't feel guilty about it. It's also helpful to remember that if a simple statement or gesture could fix it, we would have done it by now.

2. **Crying is normal.**
   Crying is a healthy response to emotional pain. Suppressed grief leads to complications. As talking and crying go hand in hand, the bereaved need the gift of listening every single day.

3. **Grief is an emotional wound.**
   Think of it as a severe injury to our heart. For this reason, it is helpful to think of us as a patient in an emotional ICU. Treat us as you would any other hospital patient: with tender loving care, compassion and kindness.

4. **Grief is a long rollercoaster ride.**
   It is often compared to a rollercoaster because it contains many emotional twists and blind turns at varying speeds. It is very unpredictable, and can feel very scary. And, as much as we try, we simply cannot control the speed, put the brakes on, nor can we predict the twists and turns. Neither can you.

5. **Don't judge or dispute our progress.**
   This implies that you're domineering and lack compassion. If you insist you know better, we may respond with resentment that can severely damage the relationship.

6. **Your timeline isn't my timeline.**
   The bereavement process and timeline is unique to every individual, and we may grieve in subtle ways for the rest of our life. Applying your timeline can lead to disappointment.

7. **Isolation is common.**
   Like a wounded animal in the wild, many of us find comfort by hibernating in our home away from social interaction. If it is safe to leave us alone, then please honor our wishes.

8. **Ignoring grief is dangerous.**
   It doesn't go away any faster when you ignore it, and doing so can actually prolong it. Ignoring grief can also cause further complications such as health issues and suicidal ideation.

9. **There are many grief stages.**
   In 1969, five grief stages were identified and applied to those facing terminal illness by Elisabeth Kübler-Ross. But mainstream society applied the concept to all losses. Not only are there many stages of grief, the timeline isn't linear. Bottom line: grief isn't orderly and can last for life.

10. **Grief creates fear.**
    See chapter eleven on page 171 for more about our fears.

CHAPTER TWO

WHAT TO SAY

The land of tears is so mysterious.
ANTOINE DE SAINT-EXUPÉRY

When tragedy strikes, it's human nature to say something to comfort the wounded. Like many, you might hesitate for fear of saying the wrong thing. Words can't fix our pain. We know this. We also know it is hard for you to see us in such a broken state. In this chapter you'll find a list of the best things to say and why, along with statements the writers found most soothing or helped them generally feel more supported.

What happens if you say nothing at all? If you avoid reaching out for fear of saying the wrong thing, your silence becomes the elephant in the room. Or worse, it can send the unintentional message that we should be over it by now. Or that we're not important enough for you to stop what you're doing to reach out.

Though these signals are seldom intended, that is often how they are perceived. We will remember who was there in our time of need, and those who faded into the background. So we offer you the following list of the best things to say, and why. Always remember that if all else fails, you can never go wrong with a heartfelt hug.

HOW WE THINK GRIEF WORKS

HOW GRIEF ACTUALLY WORKS

Best Things to Say (and Why)

🌼 **"I'm so very sorry." And then stay quiet.**
This statement says you respect our sorrow without trying to fix it. It also reassures us that you feel safe for us to be around, that you won't try to guide or criticize our journey.

🌼 **"Would you like to talk? I'm a good listener."**
The ability to talk openly about our loved one is critical to our recovery. It's even better if we can do it without parameters. Listen to us ramble, alternate between tears and laughter, jump topics and repeat ourselves without judgment. Just listen.

🌼 **"I'm going to the grocery store. Can I bring you toilet paper?"**
We're too overwhelmed to know what we need. Further, our minds are very muddled, and even simple decision-making becomes very difficult. Offering concise choices reduces the effort needed to make decisions. Use your own errand list as an example of what we might need.

🌼 **"I would love to hear more about _____ (the deceased)."**
Many people find it uncomfortable bringing up our loved one for fear it will cause us more pain. But our loved one is the only thing we can think about every second of the day. The invitation to share our loved one allows us to ease the one-person dialogue going on in our head. Further, sharing our loved one with you helps us to process the loss. The more we are allowed to process the loss, the better for our recovery.

🌼 **"I heard that feeling crazy is common."**
Grieving can be very scary, and we often feel like we're losing control. This statement offers reassurance that our wild emotions are normal, and gives us hope that it is survivable.

🌼 **Say our loved one's name.**
See above. It doesn't cause us more pain, and we love hearing it.

🌼 **Prayers are comforting for some.**
Those with steadfast faith find prayers to be very comforting. But reciting prayers and Scripture is helpful only if <u>we</u> are of strong faith, not you. This isn't the time to convert us.

🌸 **Ask concrete questions.**
Some questions are too generic, like "How are you doing?" or "Are you getting much sleep?" Instead, ask something specific such as, "Would you like me to watch the kids so you can take a nap?"

🌸 **If all else fails and you can't remember the above, say nothing.**
The truth is that we won't remember what you say, but we will remember you being by our side in our darkest hour. So remember this easy motto: Listen. Hug. Repeat.

More Suggestions

🌸 "_____ was a wonderful person, and will be greatly missed."

🌸 "_____ was very special to me, too. I'm so very sorry."

🌸 "I can't imagine what you're feeling."

🌸 "I don't know what your religious belief is, or if you have one, but please know I'm praying for your comfort."

🌸 "I'm here for you."

🌸 "When you need to talk, I'm available 24/7."

🌸 "I wish I could lessen your pain."

🌸 "My heart hurts for you."

🌸 "Tell me about your loved one."

🌸 "Would you like to go for a walk/movie/dinner?"

🌸 Share a story about our loved one.

🌸 Offer comforting song lyrics.

🌸 Listen. Hug. Repeat.

Forget Me Nots

1. **Say their name.**
   Don't avoid our loved one's name. We love hearing it.

2. **We need to talk about our loved one.**
   Don't change the subject if we bring our loved one's name up in conversation. Talking about him or her allows us to process our grief. That's a good thing.

3. **Observe our cues.**
   If we shut down when you say certain statements, try a different approach. Or leave it alone.

4. **Questioning our faith is common.**
   Resist the urge to judge or condemn this. Even the most steadfast are tested in the face of great devastation, especially when their miracle wasn't granted. You can't answer the question as to why, nor should you attempt to.

5. **Exhaustion is common.**
   Just like a patient recovering from surgery, socializing can be exhausting.

6. **We're in a fog.**
   Do be offended if voice mails don't get returned. Leave a message anyway.

7. **Sorry, we forgot.**
   Our memory will be severely impacted for a while. Maybe even a long time. This is common.

8. **Our motto: Listen. Hug. Repeat.**

A sorrow shared is half a sorrow.

SWEDISH PROVERB

Thoughtful Insight

*

EMILY BAIRD-LEVINE
Emily's 43-year-old brother Don
died from a heart attack in 2004

The words that brought the most comfort were spoken by those who loved and cared for my brother as much as I did. When they shared their stories of him and the good times they had in common, I felt comfort.

*

EMILY BARNHARDT
Emily's 20-year-old friend/roommate
Hannah died by suicide in 2014

Although we all wish there was a definitive, right-and-wrong manual for responding to grief and loss, the honest truth is that there isn't one. Yes, there are general, universal words that are typically good things to say, but every person is still unique in how they feel most heard, validated and comforted. Deciding what to say can be easier to navigate the better you know the person in grief. If you don't know the person well, it's best to err on the side of caution, and use words that are generally known to be comforting and helpful.

In closer relationships, I believe that knowing what to say in a time of grief is an intuitive and learning process. Does the bereaved seem to shut down whenever you say certain phrases or do a certain action? Does he or she seem receptive and appreciative when you take a different approach instead? Pay attention to these details. If you are unsure, it's okay to gently ask the bereaved if something is or isn't helpful for them.

Truthfully, there aren't many words in those first weeks and months that will actually make the loss feel any less traumatic, but there are words that can bring comfort and validation to the person grieving, and those words are the most important. As a Christian, I personally found a great deal of comfort in Bible verses, Christian songs, and comforting literature that people sent me. I responded best to people who didn't try to fix me or wipe my sadness away, but rather chose to sit with me in my tears and love me exactly where I was, without trying to change me. The words that soothed my heart most were always words soaked in love, validation, empathy and acceptance.

*

CHRISTINE BASTONE
Christine's sister Elizabeth
died in 2012 at age 38

Statements like "I'm sorry your sister Liz died," and "I'm sad for you that your sister Liz died," I find to be comforting. I also find comforting most statements using my sister's name. On occasion I'll get a Facebook message from a friend saying something like how beautiful Liz was, or how they can tell how much I obviously love her, or some statement that is kind and nice to hear. When someone says something that shows they understand, or can relate, I find that to be comforting. Any statement that conveys understanding, sympathy or support brings me comfort.

*

ERICA GALE BELTZ
Erica's 5-year-old son Luke Jordan died in 2002
from a fallen banister in his aunt's driveway

In the beginning, there were no words. I remember my fiancé and I riding to the hospital following the police escort. I can still feel the silence and the weight of it all. Our childhood best friends, whom we had lost touch with, heard about the accident over the scanner. They came to the hospital immediately, and met us there with open arms. Our church family and friends came to my mom's house immediately. Although I hadn't regularly attended church since I was in high school, they still came. They showered us in prayer. Their presence will always be remembered. Family, friends and neighbors came to hurt with us. I only remember each person being there. Each and every person who called, wrote, stopped by, or sent love holds a precious place in my heart. I can still feel their warm hugs today.

*

SOPHIA BLOWERS
Sophia was 50 when her mother Amy
died at age 79 of internal bleeding

The greatest comfort came from those who just let me be me. They did not try to fix the situation or make me feel better; they just stayed with me. One professor at my college was wonderful. The day after my mom died, I had a huge group project due. No one knew my mom had passed away but I felt a responsibility to be in class for the group, because I was the leader. I told my instructor that my mom had just passed away the day before, so if the project was off, to please not penalize the rest of the group. I was going to be less than stellar. She said she was impressed that I came in and although she wanted to hug me, she could tell it would break me. She patted my arm, and that was it. She put my needs and me first. That was a great lesson for me to remember. I am here to help others, and that may look very different from what I needed. Ultimately, what brought the most comfort was the knowledge that someone was watching and ready to react to what I needed at that moment.

*

MICHELLE DETWILER
Michelle's 19-year-old daughter Emily
died in 2014 due to congenital complications

Emily had severe disabilities. Her care was often difficult and stressful. However she was always dressed nicely, her hair done up, and cute little blankets on her lap. People often told us that they could see we took great care of Emily because of how she looked most of the time. After her death, the compliments about our ability to care for her up to and through her last moments of life brought me so much comfort. Because Emily's care had been so difficult and emotionally challenging, it felt like they totally understood what we were going through. Their kind words felt like giant hugs.

*

CHRISTINE DUMINIAK
Christine's 86-year-old mother Ann
died from an aortic aneurysm in 2004

Four years before my mother passed, my dad was in the hospital suffering with the end stages of COPD. My sister and I were in the hospital keeping vigil over him when his brother Normie visited unexpectedly. Uncle Normie brought his Bible with him, and he proceeded to read Psalm 23 out loud. These scriptural words being read over our dad brought enormous peace and comfort to me. It also helped when people said nice things about my mother or father, and acknowledged their passing. Praying to God helped me tremendously too. Finding cards and other letters my parents had given me was especially soothing.

*

SHARON EHLERS
Sharon's best friend Joy died in 2009 at age 52
Sharon's former fiancé John died in 2012 at age 59

Because my loved ones committed suicide, most people didn't know what to say to me. Many people avoided me. Many more wouldn't even say my loved ones names. Usually I got "I'm sorry," and then they changed the subject. Very few people wanted to hear me to talk about it. That's fine. It's a tough subject anyway.

16

*

ANNAH ELIZABETH
Annah's newborn son Gavin Michael
died 26 minutes following his birth

One of the best things said to me came from a virtual stranger. I worked in a custom retail business following my son's death. Shortly after returning to work following Gavin's death, a lady I had previously helped came in for another purchase. She remembered that I had been pregnant, and that my due date was soon. With that usual look of excitement, she asked, "How's the baby?" As is often the case, shock flooded her face when I replied, "I'm sorry; he didn't make it." As I did every time this type of exchange occurred, I reached for her hand and regurgitated what my doctor had said, "It's okay. I'm young and I still have my health. I can have other children." This woman looked me square in the eye and replied, "No. It's not okay." Those words have stuck with me for the past two-plus decades and became one of my mantras.

*

BRENDA KLEINSASSER
Brenda's 88 year-old mother
died from congestive heart failure in 2011

I was told that I did everything possible for my mother. That really didn't make me feel any better, as I felt like I had failed her. I was told that I was where I should be, especially the final day of her life. That did bring me comfort. Before I left that last evening, I leaned in toward my mom, as she was no longer responsive, and told her that if she wanted to go to Heaven to be with my father and sister, that would be okay. That brought me comfort. She passed away within two hours of me giving her permission to leave this earth. I remember feeling a sense of release and peace. She was no longer suffering and was whole again. Being told that I was really going to miss her was one thing I could have done without. What brought the most comfort was when my physician told me that if I needed anything, to be sure and let him know. Even though I never needed his help, it was great that he offered.

*

DEANA MARTIN
Deana's only two children, 25-year-old Amanda
and 21-year-old Logan, died in a car accident in 2011

There were a few people with me the whole time during the initial aftermath. Knowing they were there to care for me helped. These dear people also helped me make final decisions. My sister went shopping to buy my children's burial outfits. Many people gathered at my home in Georgia, while I was in Indiana burying my children. They cleaned, painted and stocked my fridge. I came home to a warm and lovely environment, and felt so loved. Statements that brought me comfort where when people shared with me what an impact Amanda or Logan had on their life, and how much they loved them. I also loved hearing precious things about my children that I did not know.

*

DIANE MCKENZIE-SAPP
Diane's 65-year-old husband Ron
died from renal failure in 2006

Words can heal, and they can hurt. "I'm sorry," expresses empathy for the loss, and helps to share the burden of grief.

*

JULIE MJELVE
Julie's 42-year-old husband Cameron
died by suicide in 2011

In the first few weeks and months, the words that brought the most comfort were those who allowed me to be sad and in a state of grieving. I don't actually remember any specific positive words, but I definitely remember the negative moments. Just a few weeks after my husband passed away, I arrived at our house to pack it up. Without my husband's income, I needed to sell it and move to a smaller house. On the way there, a song played on the radio called "Blessings" by Laura Story. I cried as I drove; the words really touched my heart. As I arrived at my house to begin packing up my dreams, my helper gave me a disapproving look and, with an equally disapproving tone, said "What's that sad face for?"

So, the comforting words became those who acknowledged it was okay for me to be sad, to feel upset at the loss of my husband. They were also the words that let me know it was okay to need help and support. So many people told me how strong I was, and I had to tell them not to say that anymore. Because if I was perceived as being strong, how could I possibly have a moment when I was weak? I mentioned the song "Blessings." The reason that song made me cry that day was the impact of the lyrics, which are incredibly comforting. The lyrics acknowledged my pain and suffering. They do not try to diminish my experience, yet they still want me to know that there is something greater going on. In turn, I have been able to use my experience to help others.

*

MARY POTTER KENYON
Mary's 60-year-old husband David
died of heart failure in 2012

Bible verses and music from a Christian radio station have consistently given me comfort, despite the fact that the music also makes me cry. As crazy as it sounds, Facebook was a huge support for me, in that I could ask for prayers, and would get immediate responses. Just one "I'll pray for you," helps me sleep at night. It makes me feel like someone has my back. Christian stores abound with inspirational gifts. I like surrounding myself with God's promises, whether with wall plaques, devotionals, a mug with a Bible verse on it, even pillows with inspirational sayings and butterflies on them. I wonder how many people know that a blue butterfly signals hope and comfort to me. For my daughter, who lost her son, a hummingbird brings comfort and hope.

*

NANCY REDMOND
Nancy's 40-year-old husband Kevin
died of a heart attack in 2012

Everyone in my life truly, in their own mind, had my best interest at heart. When they said things like "Oh, I know how you feel, I got a divorce." Or, "Yeah, I lost my parents, and it was so difficult!" It made me frustrated and angry. But when they said "I'm here for you," or "I am so proud of you!" or asked "What can I do for you?" … those statements made me feel understood!

*

MARYELLEN ROACH
MaryEllen's sister Suzette and two nieces, 6-year-old
Vivian and 8-year-old Lillian, died in car accident in 2012

Hundreds of people attended the visitation for my sister and nieces, and most of them had the same thing to say, "I'm sorry for your loss." I know they meant well and genuinely meant what they were saying, but those words became so empty, and brought me no comfort. If you dissect the statement "I'm sorry for your loss," you realize that it says two things. The first is that the person saying it is sorry. The second is reminding me of my loss, a loss the other person cannot fathom. As time has moved on and my heart is still broken, I have heard hurtful words like "Get over it," "Move on," or "Your sister would want you to be happy." Most grievers would LOVE to be able to get over it and go on with their lives as if nothing happened. But they simply can't, because some losses bring a grief that lasts forever. It may change over time, but it never goes away. Also, saying that my sister would want me to be happy is true. But you reminding me of that only brings me guilt, because when I don't feel happy, I feel as though I'm letting my sister down.

Grievers are often pushed into isolation because others don't know what to say, which sometimes leads to no conversation at all. But most of us know that there are no words that can "fix" our hurt.

*

MARY LEE ROBINSON
Mary Lee's 63-year-old husband Pat
died of a sudden cerebral hemorrhage in 2013

All of us struggle to bring comfort to someone who has lost a dear one, and almost all of us bungle the job horribly. Canned tripe such as "He's in a better place," or "It was God's plan," or "She would want you to......." Worst of all are the "I know just how you feel, my.....great aunt Sally died, dog died, neighbor died."

*

HEATHER WALLACE-REY
Heather was 40 when her father John
died suddenly at age 71 of a massive heart attack

When my father passed away, words of advice that brought the most comfort came from a close friend who lost his mom a year before I lost my dad. The night my dad died, my friend sent me a message that said, "People are about to say the dumbest things in the whole world to you. Some of these things are going to make you really angry, and some of them are going to make you want to take it out on that person. Don't. Because they mean well, and they love you. It's just that people are trying so hard to say something, that they sometimes say stupid things. But they mean well."

*

DIANNE WEST
Dianne's 69-year-old husband Vern
died from multiple myeloma in 2010

Genuine concern was so appreciated. Those who just looked

me in the eye, and truly saw me and all of the pain, and didn't try to fix it....they were the ones I didn't mind being around. There were no words to make me feel better, but knowing someone cared enough to enter my space, to stand in my sorrow, to not worry about how I might react was a priceless gift.

*

CHAPTER THREE

WHAT NOT TO SAY

Kind words do not cost much.
Yet they accomplish much.
BLAISE PASCAL

It's human nature to communicate using words. But well-meaning statements can backfire in the emotional volatility of the moment. This chapter offers a compilation of common statements with good intentions but risk an unfavorable outcome. Please understand that grief results in great emotional distress and pain. We're often in shock, our emotions are raw, and our coping mechanisms appear to have abandoned us altogether. Which means that we're cranky.

We understand that it's hard for you to see us in so much pain, and your natural tendency is to try to fix it. We know your words are meant to be comforting, and the intention isn't lost on us. But it remains true that certain statements cause irritation, especially clichés. You'll notice the What Not to Say list is much longer than the Best Things to Say list in the prior chapter. Trust us, we wish it were the other way around too.

We do know you mean well. We understand that your efforts usually come from a heart of wanting to help a person move from sorrow into healing as quickly as possible. However, that desire to help can sometimes rob us of our need for simple, raw moments of just being human. In most cases, people will say statements with purely good intentions, and it's important to note that. However, hurtful words can still resonate deeply in the fragile heart of someone grieving.

This is such an important concept and worth reiterating: quite often we just need someone to vent to, someone with whom we can share without fear of being judged of our progress or our craziness. Verbalizing our journey allows us to process our loss, which is critical to our healing. It allows us to release the heartbreak from our soul. Bottling our fears creates toxins, whereas spilling our sadness helps to make room for healing. It's also important to reiterate that verbalizing our sorrow isn't ruminating in our loss or feeling sorry for ourselves. We don't enjoy the attention our mourning brings. Sorrow is not a choice; it is a natural reaction.

Truthfully, no words are even necessary—just a familiar, loving presence can bring so much comfort and warmth in the harsh and cold experience of loss. We often think it's our words that make a difference, but it's not. It's your love and your heart and your willingness to be available. But if you feel compelled to say something, please do your best to give consideration to what you say before you say it.

What Not to Say . . . and Why

- **"How are you? Are you okay?**
This statement ignores the obvious. And demands an answer.
Suggestion: "I've been thinking of you, how are you feeling today?"
This invites us to open up.

- **"I understand how you feel."**
This statement tends to dismiss our emotions and is inflammatory. Suggestion: "I have absolutely no idea how you feel. But please know I have a good ear for listening and an available shoulder for hugs."

- **"Time heals all wounds."**
Time doesn't heal the pain. Instead, over the years our coping skills become stronger.
Suggestion: "I've been thinking of you. Please know I have a good ear for listening and an available shoulder for hugs."

- **"At least he/she lived a long life."**
When you love someone, their lives are never long enough.
Suggestion: "Loss is so terribly painful regardless of age."

- **"It will get better every day."**
Recovery isn't predictable, nor is it a chronological process. One day can be good, but the next two might be very hard.
Suggestion: "Some days will be better than others. When you're having a rough day, call me and I'll bring you coffee."

- **"Call if you need anything."**
We aren't thinking clearly, and we often have no idea what we need. Even if we do need something, we fear being a burden.
Suggestion: "I'm going to the grocery store for toilet paper. Are you getting low?" Be specific, but not pushy.

❀ **"Well, at least s/he is in a better place."**
No matter how good another place is, we want our loved one right beside us. Additionally, this statement evokes guilt for feeling selfish about that. Suggestion: "I'm terribly sorry for your loss, it must be overwhelming on many levels."

❀ **"At least s/he isn't suffering."**
Our own suffering snuffs out all logic as to why we should be glad that our loved one can't feel pain.
Suggestion: "I have absolutely no idea how you feel. But please know I have a good ear for listening and strong shoulder for hugs."

❀ **"God must have needed him/her."**
❀ **"God doesn't give us more than we can handle."**
❀ **"It's God's will.**
❀ **"When God closes one door, he opens another."**
❀ **"God plucks a rose to make Heaven more beautiful."**
No matter how steadfast we are in our beliefs, a profound loss often triggers an examination of why our faith didn't protect our loved one. This statement can be quite inflammatory as it implies that our needs don't count, regardless of our faith.
Suggestion: "Just know that I'm praying for you. And I have a good ear for listening and strong shoulder for hugs."

❀ **"You need to stay strong for_____"**
❀ **"You are so strong!"**
Both of these evoke guilt for wanting to cry. Suppressed sorrow leads to complications that not only hinder our ability to recover, but creates confusion over why we feel so weak.
Suggestion: "You don't need to stay strong."
Suggestion: "We will be strong for you."

❀ **"I miss him/her as much as you do."**
This dismisses our sorrow and implies competition for the loss.
Suggestion: "I miss them too."

🕊 **"It's time to move on."**
This implies that you know what's better for us than we do. Rushing through it can hinder long-term recovery.
Suggestion: None.

🕊 **"We all lose someone at some point," or "Loss is a part of life."**
While both statements are true, they lack compassion and dismiss one's right to move through the bereavement process.
Suggestion: "Loss is so terribly hard!"

🕊 **"You can have another child."**
One person doesn't replace another. Also, while in great emotional distress, we are virtually incapable of looking ahead.
Suggestion: None.

🕊 **"You'll find someone else."**
Again, one person doesn't replace another. And looking to the future will feel too scary for a while.
Suggestion: None.

🕊 **"I hear they are finding a cure for that now."**
This adds disappointment and jealousy that a cure wasn't found in time to save our loved one.
Suggestion: "Are you going to continue your involvement with the organization for the disease your loved one had?"

🕊 **"Why didn't the doctor suggest you go to the hospital?"**
We don't know why.
Suggestion: "What type of choices did your doctor offer for end of life care?"

🕊 **"Your loved one is flying with the angels now."**
It's best to avoid afterlife or spiritual references unless you are absolutely certain you know the person's belief.
Suggestion: None.

"Tough it out.
Telling us to tough it out is asking us to hide our grief. This is the worst thing we could do. Showing our emotions helps us heal.
Suggestion: "It's okay to be human" or "It's okay to be sad."

"Everything happens for a reason."
This depends upon one's spiritual beliefs.
Suggestion: "I can't imagine how heartbreaking this must be."

"At least they're aren't suffering anymore."
While intellectually true, this doesn't change our need to process the loss.
Suggestion: None.

"They would want you to be happy."
Sometimes feeling happy isn't possible, so this generates guilt.
Suggestion: None.

Also avoid . . .

- "Your children need you."
- "It gets better with time."
- "You'll be okay."
- "You're young; you can have more children."
- "Take care of yourself."
- "Think positive thoughts."
- "Appreciate what you had."
- "You're doing so well!"
- "You knew it was coming. You shouldn't be so upset."
- "Stop being so weak."

Forget Me Nots

1. **Crying is normal.**
    Spilling our sadness helps make room for the healing.

2. **Words can't heal a broken heart. Some make it worse.**
    If you find yourself struggling to say something, say nothing at all. Just listen, hug, repeat.

3. **Avoid clichés.**
    Please, and thank you.

4. **Logic doesn't work.**
    We wish it did.

5. **Staying strong is not realistic.**
    Nor is it healthy for us. Crying is cleansing.

6. **Grief isn't predictable.**
    Nor is it a chronological process.

7. **Grief doesn't have a timeframe.**
    Because every loss is unique, so is the healing process and recovery time. Some losses never heal.

8. **Hugs are priceless.**
    No words are needed. Just offer a heartfelt hug.

9. **Guilt doesn't work.**
    Any statement that makes us feel guilty for crying or grieving creates additional angst.

Sometimes, when I tell you

"I'm

ANXIOUS   HURTING   APATHETIC

SCARED

SAD   DRAINED   LONELY   DYSFUNCTIONAL   WEARY   EXHAUSTED   LOST

HOPELESS   STRESSED

FINE"

I wish you would read between the lines.

Thoughtful Insight

*

EMILY BAIRD-LEVINE
Emily's 43-year-old brother Don
died from a heart attack in 2004

People are at a loss for what to say when someone is grieving, so they often say things that are not of comfort. Perhaps they mean well, but are having their own struggles or have not experienced a loss, and really are unfamiliar with what would be appropriate. "It will get better." No, it doesn't get better. It gets different, but not better. Alternative: "I know this is difficult and I hope it gets less painful over time." Another painful statement is, "Move on." Continuing with daily life is one thing, but moving on from the loss doesn't happen. We are forever changed. Alternative: "Take it one day at a time." Finally, "He had a good life." Yes, but I wanted him to have a longer, good life. Alternative: "It must be so painful to lose a brother at any age."

*

EMILY BARNHARDT
Emily's 20-year-old friend/roommate
Hannah died by suicide in 2014

As a Christian, I noticed a handful of misguided approaches toward grief in the Christian community, as well. As Christians, our knowledge of eternity in heaven is our greatest hope and what we look forward to most. We can rejoice in knowing that those who've gone to heaven before us will be there to greet us when our time comes. Yet, believing we will one day see our loved one again does not take away the pain of losing them for the rest of our life here on earth. Our hope of heaven should never desensitize us to the depth of pain someone else feels. We often want so badly to bring relief to

31

hurting hearts, so we pull out every empowering Bible verse, every positive biblical truth, and every promise of God in our attempt to turn that person's sorrow into hope. But we don't know God's specific plan, so we can't accurately decipher what seasons of grief a person should or shouldn't go through, and how long it should last. God fashioned our hearts with the capacity to feel deep emotions, and since grief is a deeply emotionally-based experience, we can then see that grief isn't sinful or wrong. Cheery biblical truths and happy promises of God will remain concrete and alive, whether we voice them to the bereaved or not.

So, while we should always try to encourage and uplift others in grief, we should also be sensitive and discerning toward our timing and delivery. Lastly, sorrow and hope can and do coexist. Some of the greatest and most powerful confessions of hope in the Bible are spoken from the deepest pits of human sorrow.

*

ERICA GALE BELTZ
Erica's 5-year-old son Luke Jordan died in 2002
from a fallen banister in his aunt's driveway

When someone shares that they lost a child, unless you know them well, do not ask them to relive the details of their child's death. Luke's death became harder to talk about, and the darkness started to set in. I had a difficult time forming sentences and having normal conversations. In places like the supermarket, I just couldn't escape the small talk. When a random stranger would ask, "Do you have children?" At first I bravely told the truth, "Yes," I replied. "I have two. One is in Heaven and one is here on earth." But each time I became hysterical and ran out of the store. Please don't tell me: (1) this is God's will, (2) God doesn't give us more than we can handle, or (3) God must have needed another angel. This isn't the right time.

*

SOPHIA BLOWERS
Sophia was 50 when her mother Amy
died at age 79 of internal bleeding

I found it very stressful to have people tell me what to do or how to feel. I had so many people tell me that I needed to get rid of mom's stuff, clean out her room, wash all of her clothing. I did need to do all of those things, when I was ready. It made me want to scream when people told me how to grieve. If you do X, you will feel better. The problem is that no one can tell another person what will make him or her feel better. And there will be parts of us that never truly feel better. This is my path, my time frame for healing; I need to be in control of it.

*

LYNDA CHELDELIN FELL
Lynda's 15-year-old daughter Aly
died in a car accident in 2009

There are a number of well-meaning phrases that grated on my nerves. "At least you have other children," was one of them. If your arm is amputated suddenly without anesthesia, the sheer agony makes it impossible to be thankful for having a second arm. Of course you're thankful, that goes without saying. But the overwhelming pain clouds all analytical thoughts.

The one phrase I hated to the point of rage was "You are so strong!" Meant to be a compliment, it instantly raised my blood pressure to an alarming level. I *looked* strong simply because I took great effort for the benefit of everyone else; because it was hard for people to see me such a mess. But the effort required to *look* normal, even just to get groceries, exhausted my resources for the rest of the day. Which meant that by the time I returned home, I had no coping skills left. Inside my head, I felt like a hot mess, and more than a little crazy. So then I felt like an impostor. I felt caught in a game of charades, and I had no choice; I had to play to make others less uncomfortable around me. And that made me angry. I took it out in the weirdest ways, like cart rage in the grocery store. Oh, I had cart rage for the longest time! So please spare yourself possible cart rage by other bereaved individuals and refrain from saying, "You are so strong."

*

MICHELLE DETWILER
Michelle's 19-year-old daughter Emily
died in 2014 due to congenital complications

There were words that felt like people had no idea what they were talking about. They said things like, "Well, she has her wings now!" Or, "She's flying with the angels now." I didn't want to hear about Emily flying with angels, or her having wings. My Protestant Christian beliefs do not agree with those statements. Emily isn't an angel now. I would either smile and try to ignore what they said or, through my tears, tell the person how I felt and what I knew to be true. Emily was in heaven enjoying her new home. I do believe she is running, jumping on beds and singing. She is also eating dinner with Jesus! There are no wings for her, she isn't an angel, she is a person who is much loved by her family and by Jesus!

*

CHRISTINE DUMINIAK
Christine's 86-year-old mother Ann
died from an aortic aneurysm in 2004

Anything that might have been negatively said about my loved one, even if it were said in a joking manner, would be very hurtful. It would be very appreciated if you could find something kind or nice to say about the person's loved one.

34

*

SHARON EHLERS
Sharon's best friend Joy died in 2009 at age 52
Sharon's former fiancé John died in 2012 at age 59

Most people didn't know what to say, and therefore, avoided me. Saying something is better than saying nothing at all. I wish they had just admitted they didn't know what to say, or had shared memories of my loved ones; it would have really helped me.

*

ANNAH ELIZABETH
Annah's newborn son Gavin Michael
died 26 minutes following his birth

The phrase "You're young, you can have more children," made me feel hopeful that I had youth on my side, but it also made me angry because I recognized the truth that youth wasn't the only controlling factor. I was twenty-five years old, and my son died, and I was twenty-six years old when I had my miscarriage. Sometimes I wanted to scream, "Talk to me, again, about youth!"

"I'm here if you need me," was another string of words that took its toll. What I now realize is that, just like everything else in life, sometimes people are sincere, and sometimes they're not. The other piece I realized is that, even if the person meant what she said, sometimes she wasn't prepared for the type of help I needed. Both of these messages made me feel that I should somehow be thankful for my tragedy.

*

DEANA MARTIN
Deana's only two children, 25-year-old Amanda
and 21-year-old Logan, died in a car accident in 2011

Try to avoid saying much at all. Words are not necessary, and will most likely not be remembered by the bereaved, unless you say the wrong things, those might stick. "Try to avoid the typical platitudes: These sayings don't help.

*

DIANE MCKENZIE-SAPP
Diane's 65-year-old husband Ron
died from renal failure in 2006

The words, "It gets better with time," grated. I cried, "What is going to be better in three months? In six months? Me? I doubt it. Ron? He's dead, and he will still be dead. Just tell me what the heck is going to be better?" I spoke those words thinking that such a response was realistic, but it was anger speaking. Acceptance is found in the serenity prayer: God grant me the serenity to accept what I cannot change, the courage to change what I can, and the wisdom to know the difference. Accepting was the easy part, but what change was I responsible for? What could I possibly change?

*

JULIE MJELVE
Julie's 42-year-old husband Cameron
died by suicide in 2011

There were quite a few thing that people inadvertently said that were really not helpful. One of them was when people said "Call me if you need anything." When we're in the midst of grief, we're tired and worn out. The funeral is not the end of our struggles. There is still a lot of paperwork to be done and belongings to pack away. One of the hardest things to do is find the time and energy to pick up the phone and call someone to see if they can help. It is better to simply call and offer assistance. It takes much less energy to pick up a phone which is already ringing, and accept a concrete offer for help. Another statement that was not helpful for me was "You're so strong." It sounds like a compliment, and I'm sure it was so meant well. However, telling me that I'm strong makes me feel like now I can't show any weakness. Now I MUST be strong at all times. And I'm definitely not. I am tired. I am sad. I am full of weakness. Please allow me to be that way. Please stand beside me, hold me up though this difficult time, but please don't ask me to be strong all of the time. It does not help me.

*

MARY POTTER KENYON
Mary's 60-year-old husband David
died of heart failure in 2012

I hated to hear "Take care of yourself," because as a mother of eight children, I never really did learn to take care of myself. How was I supposed to do that after I lost my husband? I wish I could have said what I was thinking, which was "Really? How? How am I to take care of myself, much less these girls I still have at home?" Why didn't anyone think I might need a little taking care of? My husband was my rock. He kept me balanced when I was feeling anxious or worried, and now he was gone." Another comment that bothered me was "You are doing so well." Sometimes, it felt like an accusation, that I must not have loved David enough to fall apart. But honestly, I wasn't doing very well. I still have days when I wish someone would just give me a hug and ask me how I am really doing, and be willing to hear the honest truth.

*

NANCY REDMOND
Nancy's 40-year-old husband Kevin
died of a heart attack in 2012

I have equated this grief journey with being in a snow globe that has been shaken to the point where so much stuff flying around me that I don't know which end is up. I will find my equilibrium, I promise. I will do the things you "think" I should do, like sharing my husband's belongings or getting a new car or, God forbid, date again, if that is in my future. For now? I'm doing the best I can, and I am working toward the same goals you have for me but at my own pace. I know you're there. I promise to reach out for your hand if I should fall, but understand this is my journey. If I follow the advice of others and do things before I am ready to do so, I may become bitter or disappointed in the end. Let me do this.

When people remind me that I still have loved ones around who love me and want to be with me, I feel like Kevin's life and my grief are somehow being diminished or "invalidated." Also, please don't tell me I need to get past this. I don't know how, and it may never happen. I don't have an instruction manual on this journey. Many days I feel like I am walking blindfolded. Please don't compare my grief to your friend whose husband or wife also passed away. We are different people. We shared different marriages. We shared different love stories. Do not tell me I should seek counseling. I have done so and by the time I was done, my counselor told me I was teaching her more about coping than she could ever teach me. Don't tell me I'm young and I will find someone new. That is the furthest thing from my mind. I have already had the best husband, and to suggest that there could be someone else in my future feels like I am betraying my marriage.

*

MARYELLEN ROACH
MaryEllen's sister Suzette and two nieces, 6-year-old
Vivian and 8-year-old Lillian, died in car accident in 2012

Grief is very personal and unique to each individual griever. Emotions run high, so it becomes very upsetting when others tell me how I should or shouldn't grieve. Each person has to grieve their own way, so they're able to heal. My dad and little sister find it comforting to look at pictures of Suzette and the girls, but neither my mom nor I can handle it, so we all just allow each other to do what we feel is best for us individually. Fortunately for me, my family and most of my friends have been very supportive; however, friends of mine have had horribly hurtful things said to them. I feel the hurtful comments are generally said by people who just do not understand what grief is like.

*

MARY LEE ROBINSON
Mary Lee's 63-year-old husband Pat
died of a sudden cerebral hemorrhage in 2013

People I wanted to smack said things like "I know how you feel; I lost my dog." Or, "He's in a better place." A better place is right next to me.

"He would have wanted you to: _____." How the hell do you know what my husband wanted?

"Are you going to stop wearing your rings?" What's it to you?

"When are you going to start dating?" Again, what's it to you? Partly because of this pressure, I *did* date again. It was disastrous, and I'm sorry I ever did. It's none of your business.

Any sentence that began with "I think you should...."

Pretty much anything you say after "I'm sorry for your loss," is unhelpful and possibly harmful. Shut up! Give me a hug! Shut up again! Give me a hug again! Now you get the idea!

*

HEATHER WALLACE-REY
Heather was 40 when her father John
died suddenly at age 71 of a massive heart attack

While we tell people that there are no right words for people coping with grief, there are certainly a few WRONG words. "God gives his biggest struggles to his strongest soldiers." You don't care how strong you are, or what God has given you at this point. You just want the person back. Instead say: "I am sorry for your loss."

Another statement to avoid is "God never gives us more than we can handle." If you read the Bible, God routinely sees people through things that are MUCH more than they can handle. This is akin to saying "You'll get through this." Instead say: "I will be here for you, no matter when you need to talk, even if it's 4 a.m."

"It's part of God's plan." This is one of my least favorites. I do not believe in a God who rips the ones we love away from us, and all this statement does is causes a crisis of faith in the bereaved. Instead say: "I will be praying for you every day."

*

DIANNE WEST
Dianne's 69-year-old husband Vern
died from multiple myeloma in 2010

Unless you've experienced a devastating loss, you truly cannot understand what your bereaved friend is feeling. And even then, your loss is not the same as their loss. Please don't make comparisons. One loss is not better or worse than another. It is OUR loss, that is all that matters. I kept up a façade when out in public or at work, which caused people to regularly comment about how "strong" I was. I grew to hate that word.

"I know exactly how you feel." No, you do not.

"How are you?" Oh my ... how do you think I am?

"You are so strong." I'm not feeling strong at all.

"Let me know what you need." I won't call you. I don't know what I need – and even if I do, I won't ask.

"He's in a better place." The best place for him to be is here with me.

"You can rest now." If they were a caregiver, understand they may need to grieve the loss of that role right along with the loss of their loved one.

"You should do ...." (fill in the blank). Grief can't be fixed so please don't share what you think I should be doing.

*

CHAPTER FOUR

WHAT TO DO

Only do what
your hearts tells you.
PRINCESS DIANA

There are so many opportunities to help someone in the aftermath, and the only limitation is your imagination. The gestures recommended in this chapter are suggestions to use as a guideline only as you consider our needs. Does our family live out of state, making help in short supply? Are we already under a financial strain, and can't afford extra toilet paper to serve the visitors stopping by to pay their respects? Do our children need a ride to soccer practice or piano lessons? Do we have a living room full of medical equipment that needs to be returned?

Many well-meaning support people say, "Call me if you need anything." We often fear being a burden, or we aren't comfortable asking for help. Both of these situations hinder us from reaching out. Or we're simply too exhausted to find the phone. Further, our brain is in a fog that clouds everything, including memory and judgment; we're existing on autopilot. Remembering who offered to take Johnny to soccer practice is nearly impossible. Even when you look us in the eye while slowly and firmly saying, "I can take

Johnny to soccer practice tomorrow," we still won't remember. Even if we nod and smile. It's part of the grieving process, and we have no control over it, try as we might. Which means don't make assumptions based on appearances. We may look in control. We may look like we're doing okay. But we're not. Simple truth.

Finally, one of the key things to remember is to offer only the help you can provide, and without expectation for being entertained when you do. When we accept help, we are often relying on and looking forward to whatever assistance you offered. Also, no matter how small you perceive an act of kindness to be, chances are it will bring a huge relief and will ripple through our hearts for years to come.

What To Do

🌸 **Attend the service.**
Don't let fear keep you away. Go and offer a heartfelt hug.

🌸 **Spend time with the family.**
Don't let fear keep you away. Even if you haven't seen us in years.

🌸 **Keep us fueled.**
Call the funeral home to see if beverage service is provided for our family. Send trays of sandwiches or fruit to the viewing so our family can keep our energy up throughout the day.

🌸 **Take care of our children.**
Offer to watch the children so we can accomplish what needs to be done or take a much-needed nap. Or better yet, drive the kids to practice and buy them a milkshake on the way.

🌸 **Consider our needs.**
Instead of flowers, give stamps for all the thank-you cards.

🌸 **Bring or send groceries.**
Eating is the farthest thing from our mind, but children and visitors still need to eat. Deliver a meal in disposable, non-returnable containers so we don't have to remember who needs pans replaced when the original gets lost in the shuffle.

🌸 **Unexpected expenses.**
Send a Wal-Mart gift card to ease financial burden of needing to buy unexpected supplies.

🌸 **Look around.**
Chores are piling up. Wash dishes or do laundry. Please.

🌸 **Check on us.**
Send a quick text without expecting a response. It warms our heart to know you're thinking of us.

Long distance.
If you live out of state, send a care package.

Share freely.
Share memories of our loved one. It's like music to our ears.

Drop and run.
Deliver supplies without expectations of being entertained.

A little TLC.
Gift us with a comfort item, such as chocolate, body wash or a scented candle.

Our pets.
Feed our four-legged family members to alleviate one daily chore.

Run interference for us.
Answer the door, arrange meals or help with mundane chores. Don't wait to be asked.

They're so pretty, but....
Divide the memorial flowers after the service. The smell can be overwhelming in our home.

Thank-you cards.
Help write them out, seal them shut, apply postage and mail.

Care packages.
Leave an anonymous care package on our doorstep so we don't have to write a thank-you card.

Forget Me Nots

1. **Run interference for us.**
    We need someone to answer the door, arrange meals, help with chores. Don't wait to be asked.

2. **Carry through.**
    Only offer help you can actually carry out.

3. **Every act of kindness counts.**
    As exhaustion and brain fog take a daily toll, little things don't get done and can quickly pile up. No matter how small you think the gesture might be, it is appreciated more than you'll ever know.

4. **Don't wait for an invitation.**
    We won't call. Finding the phone and dialing is too exhausting. Or we fear being a burden. Call us instead.

5. **Don't expect to be entertained.**
    Recovery from any kind of wound is exhausting, including a broken heart. If we feel we have to chat every time somebody comes to help, we might not accept your offer.

6. **We're sensitive about our loved one's belongings.**
    When cleaning or doing chores, please ask before touching or moving our loved one's belongings. We can be very sensitive about this.

7. **Don't judge.**
    Our hearts are hurting and we're operating on autopilot. Now isn't a good time to judge our choices.

8. **Should we be driving?**
    Our brain is in a fog, we can't remember things, and we're on autopilot. Or we're mad at the world. Something to consider.

9. **Say their name.**
   It means the world to us.

10. **Use online calendars.**
    This will help keep meals and volunteers available at everyone's fingertips.

Useful supplies include:

Milk
Coffee
Bread
Eggs
Toilet paper
Bottled water
Disposable plates, cups and utensils
Food storage bags, plastic wrap, aluminum foil
Pet food
Dish soap
Laundry soap
Bar soap
Paper towels and napkins
Frozen meals in disposable containers
Gift cards to chain stores such as Wal-Mart
Gift cards to restaurants
Postal stamps
Thank-you cards
Devotionals
Scented candles
Soothing music
Inspirational books
Comfort books from Grief Diaries series

Thoughtful Insight

*

EMILY BAIRD-LEVINE
Emily's 43-year-old brother Don
died from a heart attack in 2004

The biggest and most helpful gesture is to keep in touch. Knowing that people have not forgotten the loss is very helpful. Call every once in a while to say hello, to share your news, and listen to the bereaved.

*

EMILY BARNHARDT
Emily's 20-year-old friend/roommate
Hannah died by suicide in 2014

I've noticed that one of the most common things we say to someone hurting is, "Let me know if you need anything. Call me if you need to." It's a kind-hearted and genuine statement, but I found that it was incredibly hard to reach out to ask for things out of the blue. I either felt guilty because the task didn't seem important enough, or I was just too drained to even make the effort to try to find someone who could help. A beneficial approach a supporter could take is to offer specific things that they could do to help. Try asking, "Are there any specific things you need to get done right now that I could help with? Would you like to get coffee soon? Would you like me to come over? Do you need someone to bring you food? Do you need an errand run?" Anything at all you can do is better than nothing. Even the smallest act that may seem insignificant to you could bring huge relief to someone in the midst of grief. And even if you don't end up doing anything, just showing the person your willingness and being proactive in your support will mean so much.

The first months after Hannah's death is honestly a blur to me. I had a few friends who helped me with random tasks, and although those tasks seemed minor, my friends' help with them meant a great deal to me. I'll share a few examples of support I received that touched my heart. Hannah passed away during the last week of our college spring semester, and I knew I had to return my rented textbooks to the bookstore that following week. After she passed, I was overwhelmed at the idea of having to drive, find parking, wait in line at the bookstore, and interact with strangers. A friend of mine came (with her kids in tow), picked up my school textbooks, got directions on where to go, and took them to my college to return them so I didn't get charged the hefty late fee. Another time, a friend became aware of the fact that I was barely eating because I couldn't even get myself to go to the grocery store. So with no warning, she unexpectedly left a huge bag of groceries on my doorstep one morning. I was so deeply touched at her simply wanting to do something small to make my day a little bit less overwhelming. And when I saw those groceries, I literally cried, because it meant that much to me.

A week or two after Hannah's death one of my friend's came over. We were good friends, but hadn't really spent much one-on-one time together. She came to my apartment just to be with me for a little while. She sat with me while I cried. She cried with me, and listened to me pour out my heart. She empathized and validated what I was feeling. She didn't try to offer any special healing words. I don't even think she gave me any advice at all. And I'm glad; no advice was needed. What I deeply needed was exactly what she gave me, and that's why I'll never forget that memory.

We should always be aware that words can sometimes actually do more harm than good. It depends on what we're saying and the situation though, of course. But sometimes in grief, the platitudes aren't helpful at times. These are the times when our simple presence and availability will speak much louder than our words ever could. The gesture of our offering our quiet and loving presence can be the most beautiful gesture of all.

*

CHRISTINE BASTONE
Christine's sister Elizabeth
died in 2012 at age 38

I have one friend who would occasionally call and ask me how I was doing. And somehow this person conveyed it as an actual question, rather than a greeting. That meant more to me than I can possibly say. Something else that means a lot is anyone who comes to the Facebook event I have on the death anniversary. That means more to me than you can possibly know. Every comment left, every like given, every online heart and hug is comforting. There are no words to express just how much it means.

*

ERICA GALE BELTZ
Erica's 5-year-old son Luke Jordan died in 2002
from a fallen banister in his aunt's driveway

It doesn't matter how long it has been since you have seen the bereaved or the person they lost. Show up anyway. Maybe it's been several years since you talked to the deceased. Time doesn't matter, but the moments you shared do. When I found out my high school best friend had brain surgery and wasn't doing well, I wept on the way to the family home, and almost didn't go. I was afraid it wasn't my place to be there. I put my fears aside and went anyway. The years since our high school days vanished. Someone I knew from fifth grade came to my son's the funeral; I'll never forget how much that meant. A neighbor I hadn't seen in ten years wrote a letter. It touched me. Also, I would have loved for someone to take the flowers from the funeral home to their house. Flowers are such a beautiful tribute, and make such a painful day filled with love and light. But when it's over and they all show up at your house, the smell can be overwhelming.

*

SOPHIA BLOWERS
Sophia was 50 when her mother Amy
died at age 79 of internal bleeding

My best friend could not get to me when mom died. She sent me the most wonderful care package: two big jars of soup, a chicken noodle and a squash soup because she remembered we have a vegetarian in the house. She also sent two silver ladles and a fuzzy blanket. It was like a warm hug. Every time I use the ladles or wrap up in the blanket, I know there is someone out there that has my back, even from miles away. This was comforting because it was a gesture that said, "You matter, and you are not alone."

*

LYNDA CHELDELIN FELL
Lynda's 15-year-old daughter Aly
died in a car accident in 2009

Because Aly was a swimmer on a large team, our home was quickly overflowing with visitors and our fridge couldn't handle all the food. Seeing the dilemma, my brother-in-law brought in a second fridge. One neighbor brought toilet paper and bottled water to accommodate the extra guests, which I thought was very clever. The bottled water reduced the number of trips into the kitchen, and cut down on dirty dishes.

*

MICHELLE DETWILER
Michelle's 19-year-old daughter Emily
died in 2014 due to congenital complications

In the early days of my grief I could not think normally or function like I had before my daughter died. My house was a mess, and I had difficulty cooking even basic meals. When people would ask what they could do for us, I just didn't know what to say. I always told them, "Oh nothing. We are doing okay." That was far from the truth.

*
ANNAH ELIZABETH
Annah's newborn son Gavin Michael
died 26 minutes following his birth

The gestures that I found most helpful were those who somehow paid tribute to my son's life. My mother asked to place a small ring on my son's finger before he was buried, and then she went on to make donations to Children's Miracle Network twice a year. For twenty years, she honored his memory at every birthday and Christmas.

My employer, also a good friend whose son was born two weeks before my Gavin, also gave me three great gifts. Following the viewing before Gavin's funeral, I remember walking down the hallway from the chapel when she remarked what a wonderful mommy I was to my son. Though I collapsed to the floor in agony because I didn't feel like a mommy at the time — I didn't have a child to care for, after all — those words stayed with me, and eventually brought me comfort.

In the early days, I didn't consider myself a mother because I didn't have a child to nourish or bathe with love. The more I thought about her words, I began to realize that I had done all of those things, they had just taken place in my uterus. She and her husband gave us a monetary gift that enabled us to purchase a grave stone for our son.

The other thing she did that has stood out is the Father's Day card she sent to Warren, telling him what a great father he was, and telling him she couldn't wait for the day his arms were full. The greatest gestures of all were the simple ones where someone acknowledged my son and my heartache. A phone call or that random stop in to see how I was doing long after the casseroles had dried out and the well of visitors had dried up. Those little gestures that said "I'm thinking of you," were priceless.

*

BRENDA KLEINSASSER
Brenda's 88 year-old mother
died from congestive heart failure in 2011

Two of my coworkers took me out to dinner. They presented me with a remembrance angel and also a picture frame, where I put the cover of my mother's funeral program. It is sitting on a chest of drawers that you see when you enter my apartment. It is a real source of comfort. Another coworker took me out to dinner, as well. We had a chance to have a nice chat, and I did start to cry. I was experiencing that feeling that I was not good enough. I felt like I failed my mother, but I did the best that I could. It was nice to be reassured of that fact.

*

DEANA MARTIN
Deana's only two children, 25-year-old Amanda
and 21-year-old Logan, died in a car accident in 2011

We received food for months, and this was wonderful because my mother nor I were up to cooking. My daughter and her fiancé were painting their room before the accident, so it was only partially done. While I was away a dear friend organized people to come finish the painting, and they fixed up the room so nice. The same group of people cleaned my home from top to bottom, and stocked the fridge and pantry. All of this made coming home from the worst two weeks of my life easier and it was comforting to know so many people cared enough to come help.

Also, don't ask what can you do, come to my home and see what needs done and do it (with permission, of course). When cleaning, avoid touching the belongings of my loved ones, some people are very sensitive around this. While out running errands, take it upon yourself to pick up toilet paper, paper towels, tissues, paper plates, trash bags, laundry soap, dish soap. All these things are helpful, and will be used either now or later.

*

DIANE MCKENZIE-SAPP
Diane's 65-year-old husband Ron
died from renal failure in 2006

Invite me out for a meal. Volunteer to listen to a mad woman vent, cry and ramble.

*

JULIE MJELVE
Julie's 42-year-old husband Cameron
died by suicide in 2011

Offer to do basic chores like laundry and dishes without judgment, comments, or advice on how to do it better. Offer to do housework like cleaning bathrooms and mowing the lawn, again without judgment, comments or advice. Buy groceries or give gift card to ease financial strain. Offer child care so we can have a respite out. Gift cards to Starbucks for respite treat.

*

MARY POTTER KENYON
Mary's 60-year-old husband David
died of heart failure in 2012

The littlest things felt overwhelming, and the smallest gestures of help were much appreciated. When a sister folded my laundry or did dishes, it felt like an enormous burden was lifted from my shoulders. Those who understood that my youngest child would need some extra attention were a blessing to me, as well. When I think of those early days right after my husband died, a lot is a blur, but I clearly remember those moments when someone thought ahead to what might be difficult for me, and tried to ease the burden; one sister offering to include my youngest in her family's Easter egg decorating, another sister willing to sit with me on Christmas Eve. It isn't always the big things; sometimes it is the little things like a gift arriving in the mail just to say "I care."

*

NANCY REDMOND
Nancy's 40-year-old husband Kevin
died of a heart attack in 2012

Shortly after Kevin passed away, I found myself surrounded by those who loved me best. They brought food, drinks and their love. It was that love that helped me face the darkest day I will ever be required to get through here on this earth. So, don't "think" about doing something. Come over and do it. Your presence is the greatest gift you can offer. We may be withdrawn and quiet, but believe me, your presence is noticed. Also, hand me the box of Kleenex if you think I need it. Hand me a can of soda if I look like I need a drink. Cover me with a quilt if I start shaking from shock. Don't wait for me to ask. Also, be quiet with me. There is power in silence. Hug me and don't let go if I cry. Grief is not contagious. Help make picture boards if they are wanted at the services. Make the phone calls I cannot make.

*

MARYELLEN ROACH
MaryEllen's sister Suzette and two nieces, 6-year-old
Vivian and 8-year-old Lillian, died in car accident in 2012

The things that helped my family and I the most were people supporting us. Some people made us food, which helped greatly because we didn't feel like eating, let alone cooking. It was the end of July in the Midwest, which meant it was hot and humid. I remember someone made us a fruit and jello salad which was just perfect. One couple bought us a canister of coffee and a few household items, which really came in handy. Friends of mine continued to check on me and send texts to say hello or they were thinking of me. That was great, because it helped me to know I hadn't been forgotten and neither had my pain. Friends who continued talking to us just as they had before the accident, helped more than they could imagine just by being "normal" toward us.

*

MARY LEE ROBINSON
Mary Lee's 63-year-old husband Pat
died of a sudden cerebral hemorrhage in 2013

I was many miles away from the people who loved me best. Some old friends and family assumed that local friends would look after me, forgetting that I hadn't been here very long. Some wise friends figured out my predicament, and reached out in ways I will never forget, including having a florist deliver a lovely peace lily. Another pretty flower arrangement arrived, and I received several books on inspirational meditations and grief. Three years later, I still treasure them.

*

ALEXIS VON UTTER
Alexis was 12 when her father Marc
died at age 57 from lung cancer complications

I loved it when people treated me normally. That was the best thing, because I didn't want to be pitied.

*

HEATHER WALLACE-REY
Heather was 40 when her father John
died suddenly at age 71 of a massive heart attack

Some of my friends were far away. One of my close friends sent me a floral arrangement in a giant margarita glass. Another sent me an Easter Lily because my dad died the week of Easter, and another sent flowers to the memorial service. I will always remember those who took the time to send something. Also, remind us that it's okay if we don't want to talk about the loss. And run interference for us. We need someone to answer the door, arrange meals or help with mundane chores. Don't wait to be asked. Be in charge of everything we can't do right now. You can also send flowers. It always brightens the day. Or send a sympathy card that isn't just signed by you. Write something personal on the inside.

*

DIANNE WEST
Dianne's 69-year-old husband Vern
died from multiple myeloma in 2010

In those early days I just needed someone to SEE me, to look past the façade I was showing on the outside. I desperately needed to know others were thinking of me and knew I was struggling. Someone – I still at five years do not know who – has sprinkled glitter on my doorstep and sidewalk every Christmas Eve (this is in response to a note in my CaringBridge journal about finding glitter sparkles in front of our house on the evening before the funeral and feeling it was a message from my husband).

Also, remind us that it's okay if we don't want to talk. Send short daily text messages/emails of love and support. Leave a basket of goodies at the front door with a love note; do it anonymously so we don't have to write a thank-you note. If there are young children in the home, arrange a play date to give the parents a respite. Don't forget us after the service. Stay in touch – even just a "thinking of you" text message.

*

CHAPTER FIVE

MORE WAYS TO HELP

This is a wonderful day.
I've never seen this one before.
MAYA ANGELOU

In the previous chapter we examined what to do immediately after a loss. In this chapter we examine what to do after the meals stop coming. This is an important concept to grasp, because in the immediate aftermath of loss, many people rush in to help. After a few days or weeks, the numbers begin to dwindle until they stop altogether. Consider this: when the door closes behind the last visitor is when the grief journey really begins.

This is the period of time when most of us are still in shock and at a total loss as to how we take that first baby step into life without our loved one. Our lawn becomes overgrown, our cupboards go bare, our gutters fall off, and yet you'll find us still frozen in grief. Your help would make all the difference in the world at this point.

One of the most important things to remember is to offer only the help you can comfortably provide. People who are grieving, especially in the early days and months, often don't know what they need or want, and thus find it difficult to answer the question "What do you need? What can we do?" When you offer assistance that works for your schedule, you are less likely to run into problems. When your support is accepted, the bereaved person often looks forward to or is depending on that help. When it falls through or doesn't materialize, it then creates more stress, which is something none of us want.

Any help you provide is appreciated more than you'll know.

What To Do

Thank you for remembering.
Offer a token in remembrance of our loved one that carries special meaning such as a butterfly or dragonfly.

Birthdays are painful.
Send a card around the birthday of the deceased.

Anniversaries are painful.
Send a card around the death anniversary.

Share the love.
Light a candle in remembrance of our loved one. If possible, post a photo of it on Facebook for us to see.

Treat us.
Deliver a small treat with a card saying, "Thinking of you." Or show up with a treat to share over a conversation.

Surprise us.
Leave a token at our loved one's gravesite.

Don't ask, just do.
Consider the physical needs of our home, such as the lawn, the leaves, the trash or recycling.

Use your creative talents.
Make a memorable handmade gift such as a knitted prayer shawl or a beaded bracelet in our loved one's favorite color.

Invite us.
Take us shopping, for a meal, a movie, massage, mani/pedi, a soap making class or golf lessons.

❀ **Organize a balloon release.**
This is especially thoughtful on our loved one's birthday and death anniversary.

❀ **Tie a ribbon around a tree.**
A ribbon in our loved one's favorite color adorning a neighborhood tree says you're thinking of us, and haven't forgotten.

❀ **Take the kids.**
Drive the children to school, sports practice or music lessons.

❀ **Plant it.**
If garden plants were gifted, plant them for us.

❀ **Help with chores.**
Change light bulbs, walk the dog, get the mail.

❀ **Feed us.**
Continue sending meals without staying to visit.

❀ **Keep us focused.**
Help organize our loved one's belongings.

❀ **Invite us to serve others.**
Invite us to join you as a volunteer at a local shelter or food bank.

❀ **Send a card.**
Even if it's late. That's often a time when the meals stop coming, the shock has worn off, and we feel forgotten.

❀ **Send a Happy Box about two months after the death.**
Fill it with bright colored candies (hard candy instead of chocolate so it doesn't melt), book marks, a book on grieving, stickers, puzzles, magazines, movie passes, gift cards, etc., all wrapped with bright yellow tissue paper so it is fun to open.

Forget Me Nots

1. **The grieving begins when the last visitor leaves.**
   Your help makes a world of difference for months to come.

2. **Don't say, "Call if you need anything."**
   Offer something specific so we feel less guilty about asking.

3. **Carry through.**
   Offer assistance that works for your schedule. This avoids problems when we are really counting on you.

4. **Some dates will remain painful. Forever.**
   Birthdays, death anniversaries, Mothers/Father's Day, etc.

5. **Appearances are deceiving.**
   Smiling is often for the benefit of those around us. Don't assume we no longer need help when you see us smiling.

6. **We remain easily exhausted.**
   Even simple tasks like showering take too much effort.

7. **Our memory remains challenged.**
   It may stay this way for a long time. This is normal.

8. **Your physical help also supports us emotionally.**
   By taking the load off our shoulders, this provides spiritual and emotional support as well.

9. **Don't let money stop you from helping.**
   If a chore costs money, just say so. We are glad to reimburse for something that we would have had to pay for anyway.

10. **It's true that emotional pain can manifest as physical pain.**
    Our immunity systems are compromised by emotional pain, often resulting in complicating health issues. True story.

Suggestions:

Grocery shop
Pick up dry cleaning
Pick up prescriptions
Get the mail
Mow the law
Rake the leaves
Sweep the sidewalks
Water plants during dry spells
Trim the shrubs
Shovel snow
Clean the gutters
Wash windows
Wash the car
Walk the dog
Pick up dog poop
Change cat litter
Laundry
Vacuum
Clean bathrooms
Wash dishes
Change light bulbs
Address thank-you notes
Drive the kids

Thoughtful Insight

*

EMILY BAIRD-LEVINE
Emily's 43-year-old brother Don
died from a heart attack in 2004

The biggest and most helpful gesture is to keep in touch. Knowing that people have not forgotten the loss is very helpful. Call every once in a while to say hello, to share your news, and listen to the bereaved.

*

EMILY BARNHARDT
Emily's 20-year-old friend/roommate
Hannah died by suicide in 2014

Any type of chore or errand, no matter how small, can feel unbelievably overwhelming, so any way you can contribute will always be helpful and appreciated. Just the effort it takes to shower and eat regularly can be exhausting, let alone all the other daily errands and chores that normally wouldn't be stressful outside of grief. Offering to do simple tasks like doing a few loads of laundry, running a simple errand, or buying groceries, (I would've gladly reimbursed someone at times to do this) can take a huge load off a person. It also was extremely helpful having help in dealing with the tasks related to the loss. It was physically helpful, yes, but it was more importantly emotionally and mentally helpful. I was so blessed to have friends who helped me pack up Hannah's belongings, getting the physical items together for the memorial, helping me clean out her car, helping me move, etc. Also, if an errand costs money, many of us will gladly reimburse you for it. It is the physical and emotional energy we don't have to do it.

*

CHRISTINE BASTONE
Christine's sister Elizabeth
died in 2012 at age 38

It would have been nice if someone had taken my kids to and from school occasionally or provided dinner once in a while after the initial period. Anything that gives emotional support is also good. It could be something simple like saying "I'm sure you must miss Liz. I miss her too." Listen to us and just be there. We really, really need you to just be there. Call us occasionally and sincerely ask how we are doing. If you procrastinate sending a card in the immediate aftermath, send it later. It's not too late! Most send them in the beginning. Yours can mean so much because it arrives after the shock has worn off, a time when we often feel forgotten. If you are invited to some a Facebook memorial event, or something similar, join it if possible. You honestly don't have to do much. Just look at the things that are posted, like at least one of them, and say a few short words of condolence.

*

ERICA GALE BELTZ
Erica's 5-year-old son Luke Jordan died in 2002
from a fallen banister in his aunt's driveway

Going to the grocery store was so hard. I tried, but I rarely made it through a trip with groceries in the car. Sometimes I would make it to the checkout line, but then the stranger behind me would ask how I was doing and then I would crumble. Someone gave stamps in lieu of flowers, that really came in handy. Neighbors came and picked up the laundry, and brought it back clean and folded. Things like paying bills, going to the mailbox or mowing the grass would have helped. After life goes back to normal for you, our suffering is just beginning.

*

SOPHIA BLOWERS
Sophia was 50 when her mother Amy
died at age 79 of internal bleeding

Having dinners brought was wonderful, because it gave me the freedom to know that my family was cared for while I took care of a million other things. Bringing dinners that can be frozen in containers that do not have to be returned is a huge help. I did not want to do dishes, remember who brought what, or think of what I needed to return. Also, there were times when we had more food than we could eat (it was all appreciated), so freezing dinners was a huge help. The other task that was nice to have someone help with was writing thank-you cards. Even if I was doing the writing, it was nice to have a friend with me while I did it, and address the envelopes. Writing those cards can be very emotional, and having someone share the burden is a greater blessing than people realize.

*

LYNDA CHELDELIN FELL
Lynda's 15-year-old daughter Aly
died in a car accident in 2009

We received a lot of beautiful garden plants. My husband and I could hardly make a cup of coffee, so digging a hole, adding fertilizer, and planting something was completely out of the question. One wonderful person saw the plants sitting there baking in the sun, so he went to work and planted them all. Because of his kindness, the plants are thriving and are a tender reminders of the love bestowed upon us during such a dark time.

Errands that are most helpful are those like stopping at the grocery store for milk, eggs, toilet paper, pet food, medication, etc. In the early days of loss, just getting out of bed is exhausting, leaving one with no energy to run errands, pay bills, or do simple tasks such as laundry or dishes.

*

MICHELLE DETWILER
Michelle's 19-year-old daughter Emily
died in 2014 due to congenital complications

When our daughter died, we had friends who brought food during that first week. That was such a sweet expression of love! However, life goes on and in our grief, we had a very difficult time moving on with life. It was about all we could do to get out of bed in the morning. One thing we wanted to do during those first few months was put in a memorial garden in honor of our daughter. This was almost too large of a job for us in our grieving condition. When people began to ask what we were up to, we told them about our idea for a memorial garden. Before we knew it, we had a small handful of people who set out to help us achieve our lofty goal. When the dates were set, they arrived to help us work, and our memorial garden was born.

*

CHRISTINE DUMINIAK
Christine's 86-year-old mother Ann
died from an aortic aneurysm in 2004

I would have liked help with cleaning, food shopping and cooking.

*

ANNAH ELIZABETH
Annah's newborn son Gavin Michael
died 26 minutes following his birth

After my son died, my husband and I had more food than we could possibly ever eat. For the most part, it was just he and I. Following the funeral, the well of visitors quickly dried up and the many, many casseroles dried out. As I tossed out pan after pan of food and loaf after loaf of bread, I kept thinking about all the starving people in the world. A week after we lowered my son's body into the ground, the shock began to wear off, and I discovered that everyone around me had already returned to their daily lives, and that my fridge was as empty as my grumbling stomach. What I have since done is to take food a week or two AFTER the funeral, and I usually take one frozen item and another that is either already cooked or ready to toss in the oven. So many people who are grieving want to get back to their daily routines, but they don't have the energy to spend an hour prepping a meal. A frozen dish allows them to pop something into the oven when they are ready, to smell the dish cooking, and to sit down to a home-cooked meal, without having to shop for groceries and labor in the kitchen. The other side benefit to this is that it lets the grieving person know that she isn't alone in the physical sense we talked about earlier, and often provides just the right amount of company desired. If you're going to do this, a few suggestions would be to ask if there are any dietary needs, to let the person know what dish you'd like to make, and to ask if she has room in her freezer for whatever else it is you want to bring.

Other gestures that I've heard about that have had favorable results include buying gift cards to local restaurants (especially those who offer delivery or takeout), and inviting the person to dine at your house or to go out with you. Other types of assistance include gardening, grocery shopping, offering or purchasing house cleaning services, offering to entertain any children, offering to go for walks in the park, taking the car for an oil change…the only limit is your imagination.

*

BRENDA KLEINSASSER
Brenda's 88 year-old mother
died from congestive heart failure in 2011

Offer to help with errands, maybe help with vacuuming or dusting. Maybe help with laundry or folding clothes. You can also chat while doing these chores. It will make the bereaved feel like they are getting a handle on something and not feel so defeated.

*

DEANA MARTIN
Deana's only two children, 25-year-old Amanda
and 21-year-old Logan, died in a car accident in 2011

The most helpful task someone could have done for me was something my mother did, which I am terrible at: thank-you cards. She sat down and wrote out a card for all those who sent flowers, helped with the house, sent gifts or donations. It was such a weight off my mind. It would have been very helpful for someone to help me with laundry. Running errands can be helpful, especially for those who lost a loved one in a car accident and don't feel comfortable driving for a while.

*

DIANE MCKENZIE-SAPP
Diane's 65-year-old husband Ron
died from renal failure in 2006

My car had incidents. I wanted an oil change and had a $29.99 coupon. I asked for premium oil, agreed to the flush and the stuff to help my car get more miles, and a pair of windshield wipers. He said I needed mothballs to spread under the hood to keep away ants and mice, and gave me a $300 bill. Next, a car warranty specialist called and said they could cover any repairs to my car by extending the warranty. Thinking about an upcoming trip, I got the $3,000 plan that covered the car front to back. But they didn't cover a dime for my repairs, which included bolts coming off the engine block, brakes catching on fire, and broken AC.

When my tires needed to be checked, the tire man took a metal pencil thing and pushed it into that twiggy thing sticking out of the tire. With a bit hissing (him and the tires) he announced "sixteen" as if it were repulsive. He mumbled, "You need air." "How do you know how much air my tires are supposed to have?" I asked. He directed me to the driver's door, where a little information sticker on the side says "Tires: 30 psi." Who knew? Then he walked to a pedestal looped with black hose the size of a long rigatoni. Hose slithered to the offending tire, and he beckoned me to come closer to observe his technique. He punched the end of the rigatoni hose over the end of the twig thing, and with several ding dings, my tire was standing tall. Then he asked for a penny, and slid it into the tire tread, saying "If you can't see Lincoln's nose, then you need new tires." I left with a polite, "Thank you!" and new skills.

Also, under the hood of my car was a mystery. "Out of sight out of mind" prevailed. The windshield wipers whoosh rainwater into a well with holes. Rainwater drains out through the bottom holes onto the pavement. When your car sits outside, leaves fall into the well. If you do not lift up your hood and clean out the well, the leaves compost into solid dirt, leaving no space for the water to exit. Ants find condo space in the warm leafy compost. During the next rainstorm, water backs into the new unclogged filters, filling the interior with water smelling of compost and ants. Lift up the hood.

Finally, Department of Motor Vehicles won't renew a plate with a dead person's name on it. A policeman brought it to my attention that I was driving with an expired tag. I hightailed it up to the DMV to fetch my sticker but before I could get my renewal sticker I needed a new title. It turns out I needed:

- New Certificate of Title
- Death certificate
- Lien release -With the lien holder's permission, a surviving spouse or co-owner can transfer the lien instead of having to pay off the loan.
- Turn in my husband's handicapped placards.
- Lien Release. GMAC wanted me to pay it off entirely or apply for a new loan at higher rates and a death certificate.

I complied. This comedy of errors continued for weeks. I photographed a stranger's renewed sticker and made a digital replica on my computer, printed it and put tape over it. I attached it right over the expired sticker. For the next two months, I drove blissfully unaware of the legal consequences of counterfeit tags.

*

JULIE MJELVE
Julie's 42-year-old husband Cameron
died by suicide in 2011

Anything! But especially cleaning the bathrooms. I would really have liked it someone would have offered to come and help with any kind of household cleaning or laundry, but bathrooms were the hardest to get done. I found that I could scrape by the essentials, things we needed to get done to make it through that specific day-getting some kind of meal made, and some laundry done so we had clothes to wear, but to do anything extra was completely beyond me. Cleaning a bathroom was not urgent, and I was just trying to survive. So, for someone to help take on those types of chores, would have been extremely appreciated.

*

MARY POTTER KENYON
Mary's 60-year-old husband David
died of heart failure in 2012

Where were all my meals? According to books and movies, people traditionally bring meals. Other than lots of sweets, I didn't receive many meals after my husband died, and I really could have used them. I didn't feel like cooking, but then I didn't feel much like eating either. If my daughter, Rachel, hadn't come to the house every evening after work to heat up leftover funeral roast beef, I might not have eaten much beyond sweets those first two weeks. I did appreciate anyone showing my youngest child attention because she seemed so desperate and desolate.

Also, where is my village? They say it takes a village to raise a child, but I'm on my own. For those who profess to be Christian, take care of the widows and orphans. I've found some of that in my Bible study group, but mostly it's all up to me. My youngest was eight when her dad died, and in the first year, she did get some attention. But it has been years since anyone other than her siblings offered to take her someplace or give her a little attention. That makes me sad.

You see it on television and in movies: Someone dies, and the table and counters are filled with casserole dishes, loaves of baked bread, and the grieving family doesn't have to worry about meals for a long time. I didn't have that. Also, it would have been nice if a family member had stepped up to take my eight year-old places, do things with her, or become a male role model in her life. Ideas include deliver an casserole that can be frozen in a throwaway pan. A loaf of homemade banana bread can make a sad day brighter. Offer to take the grieving children for an afternoon of fun. Give a special gift that first Christmas. Let us know that you realize this will be a difficult holiday for us.

*

NANCY REDMOND
Nancy's 40-year-old husband Kevin
died of a heart attack in 2012

My son-in-law and did so much of the home repairs and lawn care for me at a time when I just didn't have the energy to do any of it. I never ever will forget his sweet face when he said, "I mowed the lawn just like Kevin did ... with the crisscross lines!" It honored not only Kevin, but it made me feel so loved. If you're in my home while I'm grieving, please take care of yourself. I don't have the energy to cook or make sure you are fed and have something to drink. If you see I need Kleenex, food, drinks or whatever, I will not be offended if you do it for me. I will love you for it.

*

MARY LEE ROBINSON
Mary Lee's 63-year-old husband Pat
died of a sudden cerebral hemorrhage in 2013

Immediately after Pat died, I was on autopilot, doing all the things that needed to be done with an efficiency that drew comments. It wasn't long, though, that a deep fatigue like I've never known before set in. It was a monumental effort to pick up a grocery bag and get it into the house. Any help at all would have been welcome. An offer to do laundry, walk the dogs, pick up some groceries and especially to feed me at a family table were things that were not offered, but I certainly needed. At that point, changing light bulbs in the many fixtures that are high on the inside and outside of my house was impossible for me. My balance was really off! Getting stuff down from my pull-down attic was the same. Clearing debris from my yard after the worst ice storm in decades was a problem (thankfully my newest neighbor helped with that). I still won't do those chores without a spotter, and I kind of save them up for when my best friend is here.

I am still astonished at how little of this help was offered in the beginning. My husband and I, and my parents before them, made a special effort to look out for the widowed, singles and elderly in our community. It was even an outreach effort by the teen group of my church when I was one of those teens. I am dismayed at how callous and unseeing our communities have become. Everybody is anxious to rush to help out at soup kitchens, and that's great, but have you looked next door? Opportunities to help are just outside your front door, whether your community is low income or affluent in dollars. Emotional bankruptcy may be at arm's length.

Few people realize too, that MOST widows lose a significant chunk of their income. Few people realize that while the income is reduced, the bills increase, as we have to pay people to do what we easily managed with our spouses. We've forgotten that widows and orphans are the original protected class. It's biblical, guys.

Actively doing things is tricky, but can be so, so helpful. Some things require treading lightly and asking. Some? If you see it needs doing, just do it. Men are good at this, sometimes. If you see something that needs fixing, ask and then fix it. I will be forever grateful to a contractor who saw my flat tire on my second car. He saw it again a week later and said, "I'll be back tomorrow. I'll take care of that for you." Other examples include cutting the lawn, taking the trash cans out and in, and changing light bulbs that require a ladder.

*

DIANNE WEST
Dianne's 69-year-old husband Vern
died from multiple myeloma in 2010

Offer to do something specific or do it anonymously; it is so very helpful during those early weeks. When three coworkers showed up one day to clean up my very nasty- looking landscape, I felt so blessed. It was a wonderful gift. Make an casserole that can be frozen, in a throwaway pan. Offer to help them write thank you notes. Show up to rake the leaves, trim the shrubs, sweep the sidewalk, wash the car, or whatever outside work needs to be done. Leave without them knowing who it was.

*

OUR JOURNEY

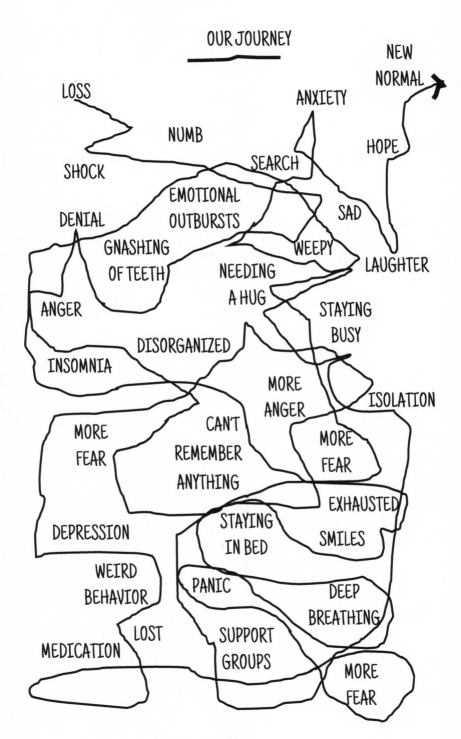

CHAPTER SIX

BIRTHDAYS & ANNIVERSARIES

No matter what anyone says about grief and about time healing all wounds, the truth is, there are certain sorrows that never fade away until the heart stops beating and the last breath is taken.
UNKNOWN

Grief is a profound, complex injury that is tricky to handle because it bares no physical wounds. And it's also predictably unpredictable. But one thing is absolute: certain calendar dates heighten our emotional volatility. Although these calendar dates come around like clockwork, most if not all of these dates will remain painful for the rest of our life, not just during the year of firsts. It is something we eventually learn to cope with. Our loved one's birthday, the anniversary of their death, Mother's Day, Father's Day, other anniversaries like wedding anniversaries, are predictably the worst.

You might also be surprised to learn that it isn't just the calendar date that is filled with pain. The weeks sandwiching the date, the two weeks before and after, are often filled with apprehension and emotional volatility which grow as the day approaches. When it finally arrives, some find it less painful than the sandwich weeks, while others find it even more painful. And next year might be reversed. We simply have no control over it. Pain of any sort makes people irritable, weepy, impatient, unreasonable and more. It's human nature. Understanding and compassion are key.

Finally, it goes without saying, but we're going to say it anyway: Don't judge us to be morbid if we wish to celebrate our loved one's special day. No matter how large or small, celebrating brings comfort to many of us. Next year we might feel differently, or pass the day quietly. Inherently, we will follow our instinctual need and do what feels best each year. Your support of our choices, and giving us the space to take a walk, collect our thoughts, and steady our emotions will help to soften the rawness.

The bottom line is to follow the griever's lead on these dates.

How You Can Help

🌸 **Remember the dates.**
Mark your calendar and acknowledge the day by texting, calling or send an email or card.

🌸 **Solitude is normal.**
If we pass the day quietly, don't barrage us with questions as to whether we are okay. We are not okay, but we'll weather it.

🌸 **Invite us out.**
Some might welcome the distraction.

🌸 **Enjoy.**
Eat our loved one's favorite dinner or dessert. Take a photo and text it or share it on Facebook.

🌸 **Take part.**
Participate in an activity our loved one enjoyed.

🌸 **Contribute.**
Donate in memory of our loved one.

🌸 **Ask.**
Ask if we have a plan you can join, or if we would like company.

🌸 **Social media.**
If we have one, join our Facebook event in memory of our loved one. Your absence speaks volumes.

🌸 **Visit the cemetery.**
Leave flowers or a remembrance token at our loved one's gravesite for us to find when we visit.

🌸 **Adorn a tree.**
Tie a ribbon around a neighborhood tree in our loved one's favorite color.

Celebrate.
Write birthday notes on balloons and release them.

Pay it forward.
Pay it forward in memory of our loved one. A random act of kindness is always welcome.

Cook.
Prepare our loved one's favorite meal and invite us over.

Deliver.
Deliver our loved one's favorite food for us to enjoy.

Sit with us.
Watch our loved one's favorite movie by our side.

Say it.
Share memories of our loved one.

Wear it.
Wear clothes in our loved one's favorite color.

Send it.
Send flowers or a gift basket showing you remembered.

A respite.
Offer a gift card to the movies or a restaurant so we can enjoy a welcome respite.

Include us.
Invite us to your home to partake in traditions, remembering that some of us have lost that in our life as well.

Remember the children.
When kids are involved, give time and gifts so they know they are loved. Even if you don't know them well.

Forget Me Nots

1. **Some calendar dates will always remain emotionally charged.**
   - The loved one's birthday
   - The death anniversary
   - Mother's Day
   - Father's Day
   - The loved one's favorite holiday
   - Most family-oriented holidays

2. **The rollercoaster returns.**
   Be aware of the emotional sensitivity you're likely to witness around these dates.

3. **Allow us to set the tone.**
   What felt good last year might not feel good this year.

4. **Do not avoid us during this time.**
   Your absence will be noticed more than you think.

5. **Do not expect to understand.**
   The dates remain painful, sometimes forever.

6. **Just listen.**
   Accept that there is simply nothing you can do or say to ease the emotional flares around these dates.

7. **Remember the motto.**
   Listen. Hug. Repeat.

A real friend is one who walks in
when the rest of the world walks out.

WALTER WINCHELL

Thoughtful Insight

*

EMILY BAIRD-LEVINE
Emily's 43-year-old brother Don
died from a heart attack in 2004

I like to eat or do things that Don liked for his birthday. Going out for his favorite meal or doing an activity that he would enjoy are comforting. Once, my husband, kids, and niece did a rope course on Don's birthday. I would have enjoyed that. On the anniversary of his death, it brings me comfort to make a donation to Don's college alma mater.

*

EMILY BARNHARDT
Emily's 20-year-old friend/roommate
Hannah died by suicide in 2014

I remember passing the year mark after Hannah's death. It was a victory to know I survived the "year of firsts." I'm not naïve to think, however, that the anniversaries in the fifth, or twentieth year might still bring up fresh emotions. Hannah's first birthday after her death was devastating for me. I felt distant from many of my friends and support system, therefore, felt too afraid to reach out. I thought I could tough it out on my own being alone all day. Deep down though, I desperately wanted someone to invade my bubble of isolation. I wanted someone to be there with me, to sit with me, or just to talk to me on the phone.

It's common for people to suggest things like releasing a balloon into the sky, writing a letter or something of the like. I thought about doing something like that, but I couldn't get myself to. I just wasn't ready. And it's beneficial for support people to understand that sometimes a grieving person honestly might not feel up to doing a formal activity to honor their loved one. At first I felt guilty – how could I not do something special to honor Hannah on her birthday? But I gave myself the gift of compassion, knowing that I just wasn't ready yet, and that it was okay

*

CHRISTINE BASTONE
Christine's sister Elizabeth
died in 2012 at age 38

What comforts me on my sister's birthday and death anniversary is to observe the day. I make a cake on her birthday and then my husband, my kids, my mother and I sing "Happy Birthday." On her death anniversary, I host a Facebook event with pictures of flowers, music from YouTube, something I have written for the occasion, a slideshow, pictures made at Pizap or Imikimi, collages, and videos of me playing a few handbell solos.

Call us on those days to see how we're doing. Mention what day it is to show that you remember. Say our loved one's name to show that they haven't been forgotten. Support us no matter how we observe, or don't observe these days. If you are invited to some sort of remembrance, such as a Facebook event, go to it if possible.

*

ERICA GALE BELTZ
Erica's 5-year-old son Luke Jordan died in 2002
from a fallen banister in his aunt's driveway

In the early years, we gathered as a family. My mama always makes or brings a cake. Her specialty cake is a Heath Bar cake. Things were financially tight when I was growing up, so you knew it was a big deal when the Heath Bar cake showed up. We had many balloon releases, and I wanted to capture these on film and in photographs. If I had something tangible to share with the world, then I felt I was keeping Luke alive.

For his sixth birthday, we had a little party at my sister's house, and then went outside after to gather around Luke's special cross. We tied balloons to the cross and took pictures, and then did a balloon release and watched them float to heaven.

For Luke's seventh birthday, we met at the cemetery. I hadn't been able to afford a marker and, although no one else spoke of it, I could tell that absent marker was heavy on everyone's heart. We left there, and spent the day at Six Flags because Luke would have loved that. His sister and cousins spent the day having fun in honor of Luke. In time, the cakes and candles made me sad, and singing "Happy Birthday" became brutal.

I celebrated Luke's fifteenth and sixteenth birthdays. Time was lost both days. Even when you are moving through the journey toward the light, time can still slip farther away. Birthdays are softer now, and I try to schedule a whole day of doing things that make me feel good inside, things that lift me spiritually. But there is no magic to help the bereaved through such a painful day.

*

SOPHIA BLOWERS
Sophia was 50 when her mother Amy
died at age 79 of internal bleeding

I am writing this the day before my mom's birthday. It will be her first birthday since she passed away. Mom would have been eighty tomorrow. What a magnificent milestone. I think I will get up and make her favorite coffee, sit in her favorite chair, and just be quiet for a while. Update: Yesterday was Mom's birthday. I spent a lot of it in bed. It was her first birthday since she passed away. I can't say that I had a breakdown; I just felt melancholy all day. The hardest part of the day was reading the text from my sister talking about missing mom. She sounded so very sad. One of the things I find difficult is when I have to remind those close to me that it is Mom's birthday. I want to scream, "THIS IS AN IMPORTANT DAY...WHY DON'T YOU REMEMBER?" I know they don't mean it but it feels like she is not important and also that I am not important because this milestone is being overlooked. I need to remember that this is my loss, and because others don't share my grief, does not mean they don't love me.

*

LYNDA CHELDELIN FELL
Lynda's 15-year-old daughter Aly
died in a car accident in 2009

As I sit and type this, today happens to be our daughter's birthday. The emotions have been building for the past week: I feel irritable, sad and moody. My heart was so heavy last night that I didn't sleep a wink. Even though this day is predictable, I always fear the emotions will remain glued to me like Velcro. I know that they won't, but fear clouds my thinking. The closer it approaches, the more I hibernate away from the world. There is nothing anyone can do to ease the sorrow, our family just has to weather it through. But some things do lift my heart, which helps to soften the rawness.

Aly's first birthday after the accident was her sweet sixteen. A group of her friends skipped school to bake a dolphin cake to surprise us with. They also coordinated a Pay It Forward, and delivered little blue organza bags filled with candy and an inspirational quote to strangers around town. One bag made it all the way out of state, and I eventually heard from that recipient how much it touched them, and how sorry they were for our loss. A couple sitting at a restaurant received a bag, and when the teenage girl explained it was in memory of her friend Aly, the couple started crying. They too had lost a daughter. Knowing that other people were touched by the girls' efforts moved our family deeply and we've never forgotten it.

Some ways that would really lift the hearts of the bereaved would be to organize a balloon release in memory of the loved one, make or buy a cake in their loved one's favorite flavor or color, leave flowers or a remembrance token at the loved one's gravesite.

*

MICHELLE DETWILER
Michelle's 19-year-old daughter Emily
died in 2014 due to congenital complications

Birthdays are difficult, there's no doubt about it. On the first birthday without our daughter, I wanted to buy flowers and give them to someone in the store parking lot. I bought the flowers, but I just couldn't follow through. I was too emotional and didn't want to explain why I was doing it. We ended up purchasing a birthday balloon, and I tied it to the little flag in our daughter's memorial garden. Also, friends came by and brought a truck (my daughter's favorite thing) and a potted flower plant to put in her memorial garden to commemorate her birthday. You can also purchase something for another person in memory of the loved one, deliver the loved one's favorite food for the family to enjoy, and share good memories featuring the loved one with the family

*

CHRISTINE DUMINIAK
Christine's 86-year-old mother Ann
died from an aortic aneurysm in 2004

I have a Catholic Mass said for my parents, as well as acknowledging their birthdays to my family. We don't do anything formal to celebrate my parents' birthdays. Tender emotions come up about them.

*

SHARON EHLERS
Sharon's best friend Joy died in 2009 at age 52
Sharon's former fiancé John died in 2012 at age 59

Since Joy and John died, I still remember their birthdays and grief anniversaries every year. I am sure there are some people who think that is weird or morbid. Personally I think it is healthy and honest. I want them to know I haven't forgotten them. For Joy, I usually wear pink because she loved it so much. Sometimes I will walk around Wal-Mart, which was her favorite store. I know she is there with me walking up and down the aisles. On John's grief anniversary, I want it to be about him and what he brought to my life. The laughter. The great memories. Pizza and margaritas. Hawaiian sunsets. Las Vegas. The Aflac commercials.

I think it's important to not judge us if we want to celebrate our loved one's birthday or remember their death anniversary. Share with us your own personal stories and memories of our loved one. Understand birthdays and death anniversaries are difficult days for us, so we will cry and be sad. Sit and watch our loved one's favorite movie with us. Invite us over, and cook our loved one's favorite food.

*

ANNAH ELIZABETH
Annah's newborn son Gavin Michael
died 26 minutes following his birth

In the first few years, all of his baby items brought me the most comfort. Our family tradition of visiting Gavin on his birthday has become a favorite ritual. But the greatest thing that has brought me comfort beyond those initial grieving years is the knowing that Gavin is always with us. It doesn't matter where we are or what we're doing, his spirit is never far away.

*

DAPHNE GREER
Daphne's 5-year-old daughter Lydia
died in a car accident in 2008

The first year, my daughter's birthday came in like a whirlwind, setting me into a world of sorrow and grief. Believing there was nothing to celebrate, the guilt monster had consumed me, and I sulked in deep heartbreak. After two years, the fog slowly cleared, and I realized what I was missing out on. The light bulb turned on. Of course she should be celebrated!

At the present time, my husband, children, and I are about the only ones who recognize her birthday. Yes, it does hurt when others don't remember, but we can't expect them all to. Some may believe it's too painful for us, or it may be too painful for them, while others believe we should "move on" and "get over it." And I've come to realize that it doesn't matter what others think, it's about our relationship with our loved one. My sweet girl was here. She lived, and you know what? She still has a birthday!

Now seven years later, on Lydia's birthday each year, we sit as a family and eat her favorite meal of chicken strips with french fries complete with ranch dressing, and finish with her favorite dessert. We visit the cemetery, and take turns exchanging memories and stories of our beautiful girl. We will forever celebrate this beautiful day, the day that God blessed us with her.

The days leading up to her anniversary date are still filled with dread and hesitation. I still find it hard to fathom the reality of her absence. The entire month silently taunts me, as the dark clouds seem to accompany me through the entire month. Regardless, come every July, on her anniversary, you will find us at the cemetery toting flowers, and releasing balloons in Lydia's honor, remembering the precious life that we share.

*

BRENDA KLEINSASSER
Brenda's 88 year-old mother
died from congestive heart failure in 2011

My mother's birthday was in January, the same month as mine. So I try to think of something to help me celebrate and will bring honor to her memory. One time I handcrafted a piece of jewelry that was half garnet and half pearl, and had a charm with the word "Inspire."

*

DEANA MARTIN
Deana's only two children, 25-year-old Amanda
and 21-year-old Logan, died in a car accident in 2011

The days leading up to birthdays and death anniversaries can be harder that the actual day. I still celebrate birthdays as if my children were here. My granddaughter and I make a big deal out of her mommy's birthday; it's important for her to be able to share her mother's birthday with her in spirit. We release balloons, and either go out to eat at their favorite restaurant or make their favorite food. Sometimes I buy my granddaughter a gift and tell her, "I would have bought this for your mom, if she were still here. But since she can't have it in heaven, I want you to have it." We often take trips on my son's birthday because it is over Memorial weekend. One year we took a Disney cruise.

The death anniversaries are more a time of reflection for me, and I usually desire to be alone that day. I watch the video we made for their funeral, and I look at pictures and try to remember each moment I can. I may write them letters or walk in nature to feel closer to them. Follow the griever's lead on these dates. Ask them what they would like to do, and be okay if it means they want to hibernate. Do something special in honor of their loved one. Make a donation to a charity in their name, have a star named after them, and then send the bereaved a card stating that this was done in their honor. Send a card, maybe even flowers or a gift basket, just showing you care. Include a gift card for the movies or a restaurant if the bereaved would like to go out. It means so much for people to remember my children and me on those days, but it does not happen often!

*

MARY POTTER KENYON
Mary's 60-year-old husband David
died of heart failure in 2012

I don't really have a tradition for marking birthdays or, anniversaries, but I do try to visit David's grave on special days and holidays. It is a sad kind of shopping; looking for something meaningful to leave behind at the grave site. I loved shopping for my husband, and it makes me sad to shop for grave markers and stones. I did have rituals for marking those "firsts." Inviting a couple over for a meal on my birthday, having a pedicure with a butterfly added to one toe on the first anniversary of his death, but I haven't really incorporated any ritual into a new tradition.

*

NANCY REDMOND
Nancy's 40-year-old husband Kevin
died of a heart attack in 2012

Birthdays and Christmas are especially hard for me, but I find the anniversary of Kevin's passing the toughest day of all. I find myself lost in memories of "that" day, and I cannot tell you in advance what the day will bring emotionally. It's a very personal day for me. I understand that others share a part of this journey with me, and are feeling his loss, too. But when I say that I want to do this, do that or be alone, please understand it's not meant to hurt any feelings. I'm trying to figure out what is best for me.

Share your memories, and remind us that you miss our loved one too. If you choose to do something special to honor the loved one's passing, share it with us. We love hearing that our loved one mattered to you, too! Follow our verbal and nonverbal cues. If we *need* to talk, we will. If we are feeling particularly vulnerable and become introspective and quiet, please don't turn the conversation into the Spanish Inquisition with a barrage of questions we struggle to answer. We will talk and tell you what we can.

*

MARYELLEN ROACH
MaryEllen's sister Suzette and two nieces, 6-year-old
Vivian and 8-year-old Lillian, died in car accident in 2012

Birthdays and the anniversary of the accident are beyond difficult. Most of the time, the weeks leading up to the day is worse than the actual day itself. The physical pain and worst heartache begin as soon as the calendar turns to May (which is the birth month for both Suzette and Vivian), July (the dreaded anniversary month), as well as November (Lillian's birth month). Every birthday is a reminder they aren't here anymore, I won't get to see them grow up, and it brings bittersweet memories of past birthdays celebrated together. The anniversary of their deaths is absolutely horrible because it's a reminder of how long it has been since I last saw them, talked to them and hugged them. It is also an awful reminder that the number of years will continue to grow, which brings fears of forgetting things about them.

Be supportive, and remind the griever that you're thinking of them when those dates start getting close. Send a card to the griever reminding them of your support. Recognizing the significant dates allows the griever to feel their loved ones are not forgotten, which is very important. If the loved ones who died have a gravesite, place flowers or something else that's meaningful on their grave.

*

MARY LEE ROBINSON
Mary Lee's 63-year-old husband Pat
died of a sudden cerebral hemorrhage in 2013

Birthdays and death anniversaries are difficult, but not unbearable for me. People dear to me have made them easier. I recommend that you remember the date, and mention it. Mark it on your calendar to remind yourself. Send a "thinking of you" card. Pick up the phone and check in with us. Invite us to get out of the house.

*

ALEXIS VON UTTER
Alexis was 12 when her father Marc
died at age 57 from lung cancer complications

Having a little time to myself, and just thinking and reminiscing of the time I did have with my dad. Birthdays were never that big in my family, but the friends who knew my father very well are the most comfort I could ask for.

*

DIANNE WEST
Dianne's 69-year-old husband Vern
died from multiple myeloma in 2010

These special dates hit hard, but it starts with the days and weeks leading up to them. The anticipation, the memories, his absence. I have preferred to spend them alone, rather than hold any kind of group memorial celebration. If they fall on a workday, I take the day off. Some have been spent taking a leisurely drive and spending time in nature. Some were spent at home going through photos. Most recently I found flying wish papers and wrote a note to my love.

Do random acts of kindness in their memory and share those acts in a letter to us. Send a card so we know you remembered that special date. Send a photo or share a special memory of our loved one. Make a donation in their our one's name to a charity of choice.

*

Tell me and I forget.
Teach me and I remember.
Involve me and I learn.
BENJAMIN FRANKLIN

CHAPTER SEVEN

HOLIDAYS

Your wings were ready,
but my heart was not.
UNKNOWN

The holiday season is a cherished time of year when family and friends honor their faith, enjoy a formal dinner, or simply spend precious time together. But when someone in the gathering is facing loss, it can create a tense and stressful situation for their circle of family, friends and coworkers. Why is the treasured holiday season especially difficult for us?

While grief itself is complex, the simple answer to this question is that we are not only grieving the loss of someone close to us, but we often feel the acute sting of past memories as well as facing future holidays without our loved one.

The holidays also brings up sensitive questions about how to handle that empty stocking hanging from the mantel or the unfilled chair at the dinner table. You don't need to fully understand the complexity of grief in order to have compassion and sensitivity toward our kaleidoscope of emotions during the holiday season. Past memories of happier times only magnify the sorrow that they're gone forever.

Once again it is helpful to remember that we are working hard to cope with a profound injury: a genuinely broken heart. Honor our sorrow by validating our spilled tears when the emotions become too raw to keep inside. Crying is a natural release of our emotions, and offering nothing more than a gentle hug and dry shoulder is the most precious holiday gift of all.

10 Ways to Help Us Navigate the Holidays

1. **Allow us to set the tone for how we wish to cope.**
   And then honor our choice. Whether we wish to maintain our normal holiday tradition, leave town or ignore the holidays entirely, resist the urge to pressure us to handle the holidays your way. We instinctively know what's best for us, even if you don't agree.

2. **We are coping with a significant wound that cannot be healed any faster than life itself.**
   It's helpful to recognize that you simply cannot do or say anything to lessen the sorrow, and trying to do so will only exhaust you.

3. **Do not avoid us.**
   Your absence will be noticed more than you think. If we ask to be left alone, honor our wish if it is safe to do so. Otherwise, include us in the festivities and treat us as you would any other significantly injured guest: with kindness, compassion and gentleness.

4. **Resist the urge to try to fill our calendar with festivities as a way to cheer or distract us.**
   Just like all healing, grieving is physically and emotionally exhausting and we may not have the energy to keep up with all the celebrations.

5. **Do not pretend nothing has happened.**
   That only creates the elephant in the room, and invalidates our sorrow. But don't awkwardly coddle us either. Again, simply treat us with kindness, compassion, and gentleness while reminding yourself that you can't fix our pain.

6. **Don't rob yourself.**
   Don't let our sorrow deplete your own happiness. Allow yourself to enjoy the festivities. The holiday celebrations are a wonderful way to recharge your own batteries, and depriving yourself serves no purpose. If needed, carve out ways that allow you to celebrate in private. Even small ways can recharge your batteries.

7. **Expect us to have cranky moments.**
   From lashing out in anger to having a meltdown like a child, pain can easily overload our emotions. Recognize that the feelings of grief are far too powerful for most to control every second, and pain makes us all cranky. It is simply human nature. If you are having difficulty finding compassion during one of these moments, give yourself a breather and go run errands or take a walk around the neighborhood.

8. **Invite us to help others.**
   Take us to help serve meals at a local shelter. Serving others less fortunate than ourselves makes us feel useful and is a wonderful reminder that we aren't alone in our struggles.

9. **If possible, help us find a way to honor our loved one's memory.**
   Take us out for coffee, and then "pay it forward" by buying coffee in our loved one's memory for the person in line behind you. Or buy a small bouquet of flowers in our loved one's favorite color, and leave it in a public spot for a stranger to find while we both watch discretely.

10. **Celebrate with us.**
    Should we find ourselves caught up in the merriment and enjoy the moment, celebrate with us. But be patient if the twinkling doesn't last long. Over time, those precious moments of joy will grow as the rawness softens.

Forget Me Nots

1. **Expect the grief to resurface.**
   We will once again be emotionally sensitive.

2. **Some holidays will always remain emotionally charged.**
   This may or may not soften with time.

3. **Allow us to set the tone for how we wish to cope.**
   And then honor our choice.

4. **Do not avoid us.**
   We'll notice.

5. **We don't expect you to understand.**
   Allow us to express our sadness anyway.

6. **Remember we fatigue easily.**
   Be flexible and accommodate accordingly.

7. **Remember the motto.**
   Listen. Hug. Repeat.

Hope is being able to see that there is light
despite all of the darkness.
DESMOND TUTU

Thoughtful Insight

*

CHRISTINE BASTONE
Christine's sister Elizabeth
died in 2012 at age 38

What comforts me during the holidays is anything that makes it seem like my sister's there in a way. For instance, I put a four inch by six inch picture of my sister in a frame, along with a few fake roses in my parent's living room (I spend most of my holidays at my parents' house). I know I keep mentioning this, but it also comforts me when anybody mentions her name. This is most comforting when my family, or anyone who knew her, mentions her name. But it means a lot when anyone does it. I keep mentioning it because I don't think that people realize how very, very important it is.

Don't pressure us to do what we've always done on the holidays. We may need to do something different this year. Doing what we've always done may be too difficult and painful now. Maybe we will be able to do it again in the future, and maybe not. But let us participate however much or however little we want to, without making us feel like we're letting you down. If we want to do things such as put up a picture or a stocking for our loved one, or have an empty chair or light a candle, allow that without criticism. Also, mention their name!

*

ERICA GALE BELTZ
Erica's 5-year-old son Luke Jordan died in 2002
from a fallen banister in his aunt's driveway

Luke's accident was so close to the holidays that they seemed to be the same thing. As all the autumn leaves changed, I could feel them closing in on me. The kids were excited and ready to make their lists for Santa. I remember their sweet faces and eyes filled with wonder. It was so impossible to pretend. I wanted nothing to do with any of it. I saw these beautiful children, and they needed me. A special Christmas and some joy was due. I had nothing to give, and it made me feel so much shame. How could I not do it for them? I knew how precious life was, why couldn't I make it count?

God must have carried us during those first few major holidays. Grief isn't over in a year or two; be mindful of this.

I came across a Christmas letter I had written after it had been four years since my son's death. I still didn't love Christmas but I no longer hated it either. "This year will be five years since Luke went to live with Jesus. We have found a way to remember Luke that has been healing for us. I am finishing up my first year as co-leader of The Compassionate Friends. I've found a way to honor Luke and work through some of the pain. We lost my Grandma Norma this year; I still can't believe that she is gone. Adam, my fiancé, had a great loss, too. His only Aunt Brenda was in remission from leukemia, sadly infection killed her. I can't explain how the experience has changed me. We would go to cheer her up, and she would always be the one filling our hearts when we left. I wanted to share how my grief had shifted after four years, and how hope and love were filling my heart again."

Allow us to take it nice and slow. Encourage us to reach out to serve others. Help us begin a collection of something significant to our loved one. We may or may not put up Christmas decorations. It's different for everyone.

*

SOPHIA BLOWERS
Sophia was 50 when her mother Amy
died at age 79 of internal bleeding

I have not been through a holiday season without mom yet. I am not sure what I will do for comfort. I really think I will surround myself with the things she loved. I know I am going to get each of my kids a gift from her. She loved to give, and I think I need to honor her. That is where the comfort will come from... not letting her be forgotten.

*

MICHELLE DETWILER
Michelle's 19-year-old daughter Emily
died in 2014 due to congenital complications

Our daughter loved Christmas. It was her favorite time of day. Yes, day! She watched a Christmas movie every day of her teen years. Our first Christmas without her felt like agony as it approached. All of it screamed her name, her life. What were we going to do to get through the festive season? Expect the grief to resurface. Holidays are difficult for many people. Those who are grieving are going to want to sleep, or maybe even run away. Hold on, it's a rollercoaster ride!

Keep in mind that we may not feel like decorating. Allow us to celebrate in the comfort of our loss. Give a special ornament or holiday decoration to celebrate the life of our loved one. Another idea is to purchase a Christmas present for another, giving it in honor of our loved one.

*

CHRISTINE DUMINIAK
Christine's 86-year-old mother Ann
died from an aortic aneurysm in 2004

Being with family members for significant dates was important for the comfort it provided. The first of each holiday was extremely difficult at first, but over time, it became easier and the new normal. Also, we do feel the spiritual presence of our parents, so we believe they are celebrating with us.

*

SHARON EHLERS
Sharon's best friend Joy died in 2009 at age 52
Sharon's former fiancé John died in 2012 at age 59

Holidays are tough, since they were Joy's favorite time of year. She loved the holidays. She died in October so the holidays were already getting started. Seeing her name everywhere I went brought me to tears. I avoided places like Michaels craft store, just so I didn't have to be reminded. John's birthday often fell on Thanksgiving. Now when Thanksgiving rolls around, part of me just wants it to be over. Another part of me thinks back to all the wonderful times we spent together.

Don't allow a griever to isolate themselves. Allow us to talk about our feelings. Help us find time to relax . Help us create a new tradition. Allow us to be honest about how we are doing and allow us to share our memories. Honor our sadness. Let us say "no" if going to holiday events is just too much.

*

ANNAH ELIZABETH
Annah's newborn son Gavin Michael
died 26 minutes following his birth

The things that bring me comfort during the holidays are the same things that bring me comfort on Gavin's birthday. At the top of that list is the knowledge that Gavin's spirit is always with us. As you come up with your own ways to help, remember that the opportunities are only limited by your imagination. I recommend you acknowledge the life and the loss, honor the life in some fashion. Ask us how you can honor the loved one. Ask what help you can provide during the holidays. Offer assistance you can follow through with, such as bake an extra pie, make an extra dozen deviled eggs, help wrap gifts, babysit the children for a few hours, offer your boat for a day on the lake, etc.

*

BRENDA KLEINSASSER
Brenda's 88 year-old mother
died from congestive heart failure in 2011

The holidays are truly a difficult time for me. Since my mother passed away, I try to go to the mall on Christmas Eve to treat myself, as I have been alone for Christmas the past four years. I call it my Me Day, as one of the things my mother told me was to be selfish. Not in a bad way, but to start doing things for myself. A caregiver can sometimes forget that the most important person is YOU. Without taking care of yourself first, you will be of no good to anyone. I always treat myself to a peppermint mocha frappe, as a source of comfort. My mother used to make candy with peppermint and white almond bark. It is a good memory for me.

If you know the bereaved are going to be alone for the holidays, give them a call to see if maybe they would like to go out for a holiday treat or drink. If the bereaved refuses to go out, do not take that personally. They may feel more comfortable in their own living space. The bereaved are still adjusting to life without their loved one for the holidays. Try having patience and seeing it from their perspective. It may be too painful to be out in public.

*

DEANA MARTIN
Deana's only two children, 25-year-old Amanda
and 21-year-old Logan, died in a car accident in 2011

The holidays are hard, very hard. I enjoy shopping for my children, and giving the gifts to people they love. This feels good in my heart, and the loved ones receiving the gifts are usually very touched as well. I can't listen to Christmas music without crying; my son was going to college to be a choir director, and I have heard him sing in concert most every Christmas song there is. If it were not for my granddaughter, I would avoid the holidays altogether and, instead, just travel during those times. But she deserves a childhood and to experience the joy of holidays just like her mother and uncle did. Talking to friends during this time helps a lot. The friends who understand how it hurts! Some of the oddest holidays trigger me into a place of sadness, but I don't notice it until it is over. The Fourth of July for example, I get very down over the Fourth of July each year, and it isn't until it is over that I realize it was my subconscious that remembered each picnic we shared and firework display we attended, and today it is very rare if I do anything or go anywhere. Some years we set off small fireworks for my granddaughter in the yard, but I don't think I have been to a large display without my children.

Invite us to help you do something for others, such as volunteer in a soup kitchen, visit a nursing home or children's hospital, and offer to read to patients. Giving to others is a wonderful way to help fill our soul. Encourage us to keep the old traditions, if we choose. If the old traditions are too painful, then create new ones. There is no right or wrong way to handle the holidays. It is okay for us to be alone, but let us know you are near.

*

DIANE MCKENZIE-SAPP
Diane's 65-year-old husband Ron
died from renal failure in 2006

Holidays are so tough. Thanksgiving is hard. Christmas is lonely now. My world is less bright and emptier. You feel guilty if you laugh or relax. I was told over and over, "It just takes time." Those words felt to my heart as if I was supposed to FORGET. Forgetting was not an option. If I laughed, if I stopped crying, would that be a betrayal of the promise I made to always remember? We have guilt for being here when they are not. And deep inside you feel that if you stop being sad and start having a life without them that you have betrayed their memory. What is a person supposed to do? Be happy or sad? Be guilty or move on?

*

MARY POTTER KENYON
Mary's 60-year-old husband David
died of heart failure in 2012

Holidays are tough. There's no denying that. Christmas will never be the same for me. Part of me just wants to skip some of the holidays, but another part of me feels guilty that my youngest daughters are missing some of the fun we used to have. Accept that it is okay to change rituals to get through the holidays. Some people want to do everything the same; others want to do everything differently. We each have to find our own way, and do whatever it takes to get through the holidays. Know that we are missing a special someone during the holidays, consider inviting us to join your family for a meal, or surprise us with a box of little gifts on our porch. Give us something to smile about.

*

NANCY REDMOND
Nancy's 40-year-old husband Kevin
died of a heart attack in 2012

Wow. The holidays have run the proverbial emotional rollercoaster for me since Kevin died. The first year, I could barely breathe let alone think about decorating or celebrating. I did, though, create a Scandinavian ice candle in Kevin's memory. I lit it at dusk on Christmas Eve and kept it burning until dusk on Christmas Day. Comfort? Oh yes! It was gorgeously peaceful and was such a beautiful reminder of the light Kevin brought to my life.

By the second year, I was ready to let the holidays kind of return to their normal pre-grief state. This Christmas is the third without him, and I find that I am honoring our love and his life by making it as beautiful for my family as I can. Still, with shopping and gift wrapping or even enjoying the lights of the Christmas tree, Kevin's loss is felt, and it feels very lonely and empty.

Please talk about the fact that my loved one is missed. It feels like the elephant in the room when you don't mention it to me. You can't possibly make me feel any worse by mentioning his name.

Please don't offer to come over and "deck the halls" for me. I will do what I feel comfortable doing. By all means if I call and say I need help, please be there! Don't avoid my grief by avoiding me. Believe it or not, your absence in my life further shatters my already broken heart and makes me feel like I have done something wrong. Irrational, of course, but your presence is missed.

By all means, don't say, "Your loved one would want you to enjoy the holidays!" My loved one doesn't get to *want* anything anymore. He's not here, so he doesn't *get* an opinion on anything!

Don't remind me that I have wonderful children and grandchildren. I don't forget that for a minute, and when you remind me, it makes me feel like you are somehow invalidating the grief I am feeling.

Please don't go changing traditions. If I have always hosted Christmas at my house, please don't take that away from me. In a world where I feel like nothing is within my control, the stress of changing the familiar traditions is unbearable. I promise I won't always be so unbending and inflexible, but understand that I need some "sameness" to hold onto during the holidays.

*

MARYELLEN ROACH
MaryEllen's sister Suzette and two nieces, 6-year-old
Vivian and 8-year-old Lillian, died in car accident in 2012

Holidays are still so difficult for my family. It has been three and a half years since my sister and nieces went to Heaven, but it's only the fourth set of holidays without them. Holidays hurt so badly because they are time for family, and there are three people missing from ours. We still gather together, but it just isn't the same and never will be. Our table used to be crowded with two extra chairs added to accommodate everyone. Now no chairs are added and there is still an empty one, which is incredibly painful to see.

This year for Thanksgiving, we invited a friend over who didn't have anywhere else to go. We greatly enjoyed her being with us, and it brought comfort that the table was full again. Of course it wasn't the same, but it was still a nice change. For Christmas, I put ornaments on my tree that belonged to my sister and my nieces, as well as a memorial ornament my friend, Christina, bought for me. It makes me feel comfort by still including them in the holiday.

If a grieving family invites you to their holiday celebration or you have always previously attended, do your best to celebrate with them. Purchase a memorial ornament for the absent loved one. Invite the griever out to lunch, coffee, a movie or maybe even Christmas shopping. Grievers tire easily, so customize as needed.

*

MARY LEE ROBINSON
Mary Lee's 63-year-old husband Pat
died of a sudden cerebral hemorrhage in 2013

My holidays, as a child, were full of extended family. Grandmother, grandfather, aunts, uncles, a cousin or two populated the merriest of days. As the baby of the family, there isn't much family left at all. With the death of my husband, I find myself very much alone. The first year after Pat's death, I spent nearly every holiday completely alone. Easter was the one that came six weeks after he died. One friend called that day. No family called, no friends visited, no one invited me to join them. It was awful! It was also the day that set me into motion to work on behalf of widows and widowers everywhere. I've had two Christmas holidays since Pat died. For each one, I put some ornaments on the tree that we collected together. I also found a redheaded woodpecker ornament that I put on the tree. Pat loved woodpeckers, and they come around the house quite a lot now, although that began just after he died. Shortly before my first Christmas alone, I wrote in my journal that I really missed getting flowers. Pat was really good about that. I received flowers from him for no reason at all sometimes. That December, and the next one which was last year, a single red Gerbera daisy popped up in my flower bed out front. I didn't imagine it; others saw it too. Gerbera daisies are spring and summer flowers here in South Carolina. These were the two coldest Decembers on record. I hope the daisy tradition continues.

Make sure we have a place to go, or join us. If we absolutely want to be left alone, respect that, but don't let us say you didn't ask. Acknowledge that you know it's a difficult time. A phone call or a card go a long way. We remember those who make the effort and the ones who don't. Don't assume that somebody else has "got them." Maybe not! Ask. Ask us how our loved one can be remembered. Perhaps a toast, a candle lighting, a round of storytelling would be in order. For a really special gift, scour your photo and video collections. If you find a forgotten one of our loved one, give it to us. We may not have it, and those are very precious. Implement the Set an Extra Plate Initiative. Look around your workplace, your church, your clubs, your neighborhood and see who may be alone on a holiday. Invite them to join you and your family and set an extra plate. Learn more at our website www.widsnextdoor.com .

*

ALEXIS VON UTTER
Alexis was 12 when her father Marc
died at age 57 from lung cancer complications

My comfort is not thinking about it, not thinking of the fact that I won't have that person.

*

DIANNE WEST
Dianne's 69-year-old husband Vern
died from multiple myeloma in 2010

Holidays are hard, and if the loss occurred during that time of year, the heartache is compounded. Those holiday TV movies that pull at the heartstrings, special memories of Christmases past, traditions that are no longer possible all play a part in the suffering. I still find the holidays difficult, and just trudge through them to get to January 2.

Everyone grieves differently. Don't make assumptions about how we need to handle the holidays. Some will want to participate in celebrations and keep busy; others will need to completely ignore the festivities. Both are okay. Include us in your holiday activities as usual, but allow us to easily decline if we choose. Provide us with an escape if we find the festivities too hard to handle. Show us a room we can use, if needed, or make sure our car is not blocked in so we can leave. Send us a Christmas card and include a special memory of our loved one.

I've learned that people will forget what you said,
people will forget what you did, but people will
never forget how you made them feel.
MAYA ANGELOU

CHAPTER EIGHT

UNDERSTANDING OUR EMOTIONS

*Joy and sorrow are
nextdoor neighbors.*
GERMAN PROVERB

In historic times, white represented the color of deepest mourning. By the nineteenth century, black clothing became customary. Widows were expected to dress in heavy, concealing clothing for up to four years following the death of their loved one; to change out of the dark attire sooner was considered disrespectful. Mourning attire was worn for six months for a sibling, and parents were allowed to wear mourning clothes for a child as long as they needed.

Today's trend is to grant the bereaved a mere three to seven days of leave. This is enough time to organize and attend a funeral, face the burial and then what? We find ourselves still standing at the starting line of our journey when we're expected to jump back into our former routine. Although times have changed, our emotions haven't.

To complicate matters, today's movies and television allot a single scene or two for grieving before moving on in the script. While most understand that this is fiction, it leads many to believe that this isn't far from truth. When we stray from the movie script, perhaps there is something wrong with either our mental stability, or the way we're processing our loss, or both.

When one suffers an amputation of a limb, the patient is provided acute medical attention to first stabilize the injury. They then are given critical care to adjust for shock, hospitalized long enough to ensure stability, and then gently and slowly move into rehab to relearn how to adjust to life without that limb. Years later, that missing limb serves as a daily reminder to treat that person with compassion and gentleness.

Although we aren't missing a limb, we use it here as an analogy to help you understand our adjustment to life without our loved one. Our wound is invisible to the world around us, yet is even more painful than a traumatic amputation and equally dangerous if ignored and denied sufficient care.

Mourning customs are no longer in fashion, and neither is ample time given to adjust. We must return to work and life without the benefit of acute medical attention, intense hospitalization, or rehab to help us transition to our new life without our loved one. Thus, our emotions become your only visible clue that we're dealing with an intensely painful wound.

In this chapter, writers offer you a complimentary seat on their own rollercoaster to help you understand what to expect from us as we transition from our old life to our new.

Forget Me Nots

1. **It's complex.**
   Grief is a profound pain resulting in complex emotions.

2. **Avoid a timeline. Grief doesn't end after one year.**
   Although the wound is invisible, intense suffering can last for years and, in some cases, a lifetime.

3. **The façade.**
   Many of us hide our grief due to societal or familial pressure to be strong. Appearances can be deceiving, and superficial conversations are not an accurate gage.

4. **It's unpredictable.**
   Grief emotions aren't planned, and can pour forth at any time.

5. **Emotional lability.**
   We remain emotionally sensitive for a few years. Avoid criticism of our process or progress.

6. **Good times.**
   Moments of laughter and smiling are part of the rollercoaster.

7. **Just listen.**
   We need to verbalize our sorrow in order to process the loss. The more we're allowed to talk, the faster the healing begins, and the less you'll be called upon to listen.

8. **Emotional pain can lead to physical pain.**
   This is common.

9. **Remember the confidentiality.**
   Treat our emotionally well-being with sensitivity. Protect it from becoming gossip.

10. **Carry the weight.**
    You will have to do the heavy lifting of the relationship for longer than you expect. Please be patient.

11. **Cognitive challenges.**
    We often have trouble focusing on tasks, making decisions or remembering details. This is common.

12. **Remember the motto.**
    Listen. Hug. Repeat.

Thoughtful Insight

*

EMILY BAIRD-LEVINE
Emily's 43-year-old brother Don
died from a heart attack in 2004

My emotions change and remain the same over time from the day of Don's death to today, almost eleven years later. I was so raw and set off often for the first few months. I could be going about my daily life, accomplishing tasks set out before me, and then completely lose it. The tears would stream freely at the drop of a hat or at nothing in particular. I would remember something sad or happy and still feel a great loss at the fact neither was possible anymore. I only have memories.

Respect our individual grief process. Don't impose any rules for grieving on to us. Listen to us when we want to share about our loss and our loved one. If you knew my loved one, share your stories about them.

*

EMILY BARNHARDT
Emily's 20-year-old friend/roommate
Hannah died by suicide in 2014

Once I started back in school and work three months after, I remember a friend asking me in conversation, "How are work and school going? You back to normal now?" Words failed me and I felt ashamed, because I was honestly feeling even less-normal and worse than I did in the immediate aftermath. It seemed that most people thought I was doing better simply because I had resumed my daily responsibilities.

I sank into isolation, afraid to reveal the ugly truth to those around me that I was light-years away from feeling anywhere close to normal. I had hoped that I would feel like I was moving forward once I was back in the usual swing of things. But I didn't. And that sent me into panic that I might never move forward; I feared I would forever stay stuck in a state of merely existing.

The entire concept of "moving forward" can devastate a person grieving, because after losing someone you so deeply care about, you only want to go backward – to the time they were alive, the time you could have helped them, the time you could have done or said the things you wish you had. You want to go back to the time when life was familiar, when you could hug them and talk to them. You want to go back to doing life with them. And the point when I started hearing some responses that made me feel pressure to be doing better than I was, was when I started to hide my grief. I also often hid my grief due to trying to match the conversations others seemed to want to have with me, many of which felt superficial. If I tried to mention Hannah, and people seemed unreceptive, I backed off. But those superficial conversations at work, school, and with friends were very difficult for me at times. People maybe wanted to engage me in light conversation in attempt to make me feel more normal, but no amount of pretending for me could make things feel okay or change the reality I was living in. The superficial conversations, as well-intended as they were, only made me feel more isolated. I felt pressured to have interesting, superficial things to say about school, work, life and volunteer activities. In reality, I couldn't care less about those things. My daily life consisted of endless crushing reminders of Hannah and her death, exaggerated by things like having to adjust to a new home that felt strange and unfamiliar, and professors at school were unaware that I was sinking under the weight of their expectations. The reminders of my grief seemed endless. Those superficial conversations that seemed to be the majority of my interactions with people became an unbridgeable chasm and disconnect that separated me from everyone else.

It was normal for others to discuss work and school. It wasn't normal for them to discuss me sobbing at the bank, having to explain that I couldn't get my security deposit back because Hannah's name was before mine on our check.

When I did choose to show my grief, I never knew what to expect. Some people would respond with love and compassion, while others might say or do something that could unexpectedly wreck me inside. Certain comments hurt deeply, and caused me to judge myself or feel ashamed over how much I was hurting, and struggling just to get through each day, and I felt embarrassed to share how I was doing. So I began to shut down and try to hide it in certain environments. That only intensified my pain and loneliness, however. Because I was then not only grieving the loss of Hannah, but also the loss of community, connection, and the ability to be authentic. I had to give myself the space to grieve more than Hannah's death. I had to let myself grieve the change, the transition, the distance from people. I had to grieve losing the life I had known, and grieve the little pieces of Hannah I lost every time something new came up unexpectedly. The transition for me was the toughest part, and I think it can make it even tougher for people grieving when outsiders don't realize that. It's helpful for supporters to give love and compassion in that process and period of adjustment.

Most people assume that the immediate aftermath of the loss is the most excruciating time period. Though it certainly is excruciating and tumultuous, the ensuing transition is equally agonizing. And it would ease the loneliness and difficulty, whether little or tremendously, if we could teach and help those who support us understand that. The people in my life who welcomed my expressing grief and validated it, no matter how much time had passed, were such a blessing to me.

*

CHRISTINE BASTONE
Christine's sister Elizabeth
died in 2012 at age 38

You never know when a grief attack will hit. You also never know what will trigger it. You're going along doing pretty well and BAM! All of the sudden something hits you upside your head, and it feels like your loss just happened yesterday. It feels like you've lost any progress that you have made, and that you are back at square one. There's no preparing for them. There's no bracing yourself for them. They are very tough to handle. And then there are the times that you expect the sadness to hit, such as on their death anniversary date. Surprisingly, those are usually easier to handle because if you know it's coming, then you can brace yourself for it. Although be aware that a lot of times it's the time right before such a date, or an otherwise expected time of sadness that can be the hardest to bear. Sometimes the day itself isn't as bad as expected. Allow us to express our emotions, whatever they might be. Please don't criticize them. We can't grieve twenty-four hours a day. So if you see us happy or having a good time, that doesn't mean we are over our loss, nor is it a sign that we don't care about our loved one or that we haven't been grieving. If you can't softly say something like "You're thinking about _____, huh?" or "It's okay to cry, I would cry too," then just ignore our crying.

*

ERICA GALE BELTZ
Erica's 5-year-old son Luke Jordan died in 2002
from a fallen banister in his aunt's driveway

The hardest time for me in the beginning was the morning. Even before I knew I was awake yet, I would open my eyes, and there seemed to be this incredible space. First darkness and silence. Then I would hear the sounds of morning or see a glimpse of daylight coming through the blinds. It was as if I wasn't even in my own body, kind of like I was watching myself wake up from across the room. There would be confusion. Once I realized it wasn't just a horrible nightmare, pain would fill every ounce of me, and the devastation would set in again. I needed to be strong for my daughter, but couldn't find the strength or the courage. I wanted to hide from the rest of the world. The pain was dark, consuming and unbearable. We were all suffering. I was given space during that time, and no one seemed to have any expectations of me. My family supported my journey wherever it took me. I started to work for J. Christopher's on the third anniversary of Luke's death. My boss welcomed me and my pain, and helped strengthen me. My new coworkers became family. I had angels showering me with love and light. My faith sustained me and still does.

When we share our pain, guilt and shame, just listen. Tell us you are there to hurt with us. Allow us to share with you our pain, in all its rawness, and just listen. Remember our lives are changed forever when our loved one passes away. Acknowledge the hurt.

*

SOPHIA BLOWERS
Sophia was 50 when her mother Amy
died at age 79 of internal bleeding

I could sense the discomfort it gave others to see me sad, so I hid it. I used the "she is in a better place" line a lot. I actually believe that my mom is in a better place, but what people don't realize is that when we lose someone, especially if we believe they are in a better place, it is not about them. It is about us. How horrifically selfish, right? Wrong! It is about those who are left behind that are trying to figure out how to live, how to breathe, how to sleep through the entire night, and how to ever possibly think about laughing again. So I hid the sadness, because I had enough on my plate without adding the responsibility of the guilt I would feel by making someone else feel sad or uncomfortable.

*

LYNDA CHELDELIN FELL
Lynda's 15-year-old daughter Aly
died in a car accident in 2009

A few months after the accident, when others expected me to start returning to the old Lynda, this was when I understood just how uncomfortable my grief made others feel. I knew in my heart that I was never going to be the same, but how could I explain that to people who couldn't possibly understand my sorrow? So I learned to put my smile on and pretend to be normal to help others feel comfortable around me. Unfortunately, it became all about making others more comfortable which took energy away from focusing on my own healing.

At some point I shut down and began to hibernate like a wounded animal who wanted to be left alone to lick my wounds in private. I started pulling away from most everybody, aside from my family. I was blessed with wonderful family who shared my grief, but outside of them, very few understood. When you lose someone you love, it is a lifelong process to adjust, not a six-month virus one recovers from. Truth be told, it's exhausting to hide grief from others, and hibernating in my own home was my solace where I didn't have to spend energy pretending to be the "old" Lynda. Because the "old" version of myself died with my daughter, and it would take years before the new Lynda grew steady enough to emerge from the cocoon.

*

MICHELLE DETWILER
Michelle's 19-year-old daughter Emily
died in 2014 due to congenital complications

After our daughter died, I knew I would be grieving, but I had no idea my emotions would take on a life of its own! There were days where I could do nothing but cry. I would call a friend; she was so gracious to listen to my ramblings through all those phone calls, especially the very early morning calls!

I often talked about what I could have done, and why I didn't do other things. In those early days of grief I just really needed someone to listen to me. Listening was like hugging me. I expected to cry, but I didn't expect to cry in the grocery store or sitting in the dentist chair! Remember, crying can happen anywhere. Grief emotions aren't planned, and can come pouring out at any time. At times, I was very conversationally short with people. Sometimes I didn't want to talk to anyone. Part of the problem was that if I talked, I cried. So I would just listen and not talk much. Each person comes back to their "normal" emotions after the death of the loved one. But each person is on their own time schedule. I seemed to bounce back and forth from normal to severe grief, up and down, up and down, for many months.

*

CHRISTINE DUMINIAK
Christine's 86-year-old mother Ann
died from an aortic aneurysm in 2004

There was no need to hide my grief from my sisters and my family, because we all felt the same way. And we really enjoyed taking trips down memory lane with one another concerning my parents. It made us laugh to do this together, and it was cathartic to do so. It was also helpful to talk about my mother to a special cousin, who was like a sister to my mother. When I was with my cousin, I felt like part of my mother was there with me. I am a founder of an internet grief support group, so it was very helpful to have them acknowledge my grief, and to have them pray for me. I did hide my grief from most others, because I really feel uncomfortable with people feeling sorry for me. I would much rather comfort others.

*

SHARON EHLERS
Sharon's best friend Joy died in 2009 at age 52
Sharon's former fiancé John died in 2012 at age 59

The evening Joy's husband called to tell me she had committed suicide, I felt like life had been sucked right out of me in that moment. I collapsed on the floor. I couldn't focus. I felt like I was in a daze. When John died, I had so many questions. He left us with no understanding and wanting answers. But answers never came. Nothing ever came. Well that's wrong, something came....extreme sadness and heartache, and it hasn't gone away.

*

ANNAH ELIZABETH
Annah's newborn son Gavin Michael
died 26 minutes following his birth

This question is like an onion, in that the answer holds many layers. I think to some degree, we all hide our grief from those around us. Sometimes we don't have the energy to go into deep conversations, so we put on a happy face. Sometimes we have pressing obligations or other commitments and don't want to take the time to share because, in the end, sharing our sorrow tends to be a lengthy process, especially if the other person cares enough and is open enough to ask questions and to engage. Sometimes the timing feels all wrong. Sometimes, even though it's not our responsibility to protect others emotions, we withhold our grief so as not to cause someone else pain.

Sometimes our grief isn't about death — the leading cause most people associate grief with. Adultery, cancer, child loss, depression, job loss, mental illness ... these are but a few of the topics that cause panic and fear in many people. "I could never survive that," they think, and sometimes say aloud. Their anxiety races across their faces, and we are left feeling guilty, ashamed, embarrassed, or we take on the role of consoler.

All too many of us have experienced that look on another's face, the person who is searching for an immediate escape route. We quickly learn to mask our own pain, and to be overly selective about what we will share and with whom we'll share.

When I became pregnant with Beauty, my living daughter, I didn't tell anyone until I was well into the pregnancy. I believed that I was protecting those people who had already endured the back-to-back shocks that were my firstborn's unexpected death following delivery and then a miscarriage right on the heels of that loss event. The truth of the matter, though, was that I was also protecting myself from all of those uncomfortable situations that I'd kept finding myself in.

What I know now, through my research, reflections and my work on helping people transition from grief to healing, is that we need to start a new conversation. We need to ADD the healing piece to the many great grief resources that are already in place. We need to know that there is something more than platitude to help us reconcile heartaches, big and small. Maybe then, when more of us recognize the hope and promise of something better to come following mishap or mayhem, the bereaved won't feel like they have to spend so much time in hiding.

Be present. Be as brave as you can be. Don't assume that you "could never survive" whatever loss the bereaved is experiencing. Remember that things aren't always as they seem. If you know a person has endured a loss, find a private time to ask how he or she is doing, or just let them know you are thinking of him or her. Remember that healing doesn't meant what happened is okay. It simply means that we can find a way to be okay in the face of it.

*

DAPHNE GREER
Daphne's 5-year-old daughter Lydia
died in a car accident in 2008

My emotions were rampant and ever changing, unpredictable like the waters of a river the first few years. After the first month, I tried to conceal my tears, as not to make others uncomfortable, as it didn't take long to realize that people were terrified of the topic. With everything in life, I always had to be the strong one, having to keep it together and support everyone else, which is a monstrous task for anyone. Looking back, I wish I would have had the strength to share my heart, and let others know the truth inside this heartbroken mother. I would have loved to be comforted and my feelings validated, but no one understood. My emotions changed daily. There was no method to this madness of grief, and I despised anyone attempting to try and tell me such a thing.

Don't try to assume we are in a certain state of grief. Don't be afraid to ask about our loss and feelings. Say our loved one's name as often as possible. It will be the best thing you could ever do. If we choose to talk, let us them speak freely, without interruption.

*

BRENDA KLEINSASSER
Brenda's 88 year-old mother
died from congestive heart failure in 2011

There are days that I miss her terribly. I sometimes go to my quiet place, and start sobbing. I miss our talks, and the things we would do together. The weekends are the hardest, even after four years, as that was our time to go shopping or dining out, at our favorite eating place. I miss the presence of my best friend, my mother. Allow me to share the pain I feel. I may not always wish to be social but please grant me permission to talk about my loss.

*

DEANA MARTIN
Deana's only two children, 25-year-old Amanda
and 21-year-old Logan, died in a car accident in 2011

My emotions are all over the place, like a firefly. What I am feeling right now many not be what I will feel in a couple of seconds. Don't judge me for this; I have no control over it.

I am incredibly numb, in a surreal out-of-body experience, and my mind is cloudy. The colors of life I can still see with my eyes, but the beauty they once held no longer reaches my soul. Music often makes me angry or sad, it does not hold the joy it once did. Now every song reminds me of my loss and the empty place in my chest where my heart once was. Because we are sometimes incapable of making decisions; it is helpful to limit our options. We will spend much more time in our head than in our body; it is imperative we take care of our body. This type of stress can easily create illness. Encourage us to stay hydrated, eat and rest.

*

DIANE MCKENZIE-SAPP
Diane's 65-year-old husband Ron
died from renal failure in 2006

I do not share easily, and I do not talk to others about how I feel. It's just the way I am. I shared everything with Ron, as he was my friend, my other half and my sounding board. He was honest, level headed, and had an inborn compass for the right direction for any path. I depended on him to weigh the merits of my ideas and advise me when I was too close to the edge. I would talk to him and ramble aloud whenever a thought crossed my mind that I thought he would like to "hear." I always felt close to him wherever I was, and didn't visit graveside as I didn't feel him to be there. Ron did feel closeness at the cemetery, and he would visit his family's gravesite regularly. He also knew I did not visit gravesides, except to say the final farewell.

I went to Ron's graveside one last time to say goodbye on a gray, misty day. I brought fresh flowers to test the new vase recently installed. Also I brought a pebble that said I MISS YOU, four sticks of incense, a water bucket and my new widow's ring. Then I sat in a misty rain, and lit incense in the four directions of a compass. I sat on the bucket talking to him, "I have come here for the last time, and I will stay with you as long as this incense burns between us." Tears flowed as I spoke to him, sitting on the upended water bucket. I spoke to him like we used to do, I would talk and he would listen. I told Ron of all that happened since he was gone, and how I really hated my new life. I thanked him for the idea of a widow's ring, and put it on my finger to show him. "I will wear this in memory of you and of our past," I said. I told Ron I felt close to him when wearing this ring, and how it "felt right." I said, "This widow's ring continues the story of "us." Other widows are asking for a widow's ring, too. See what you started?" Incense wands last only ten to fifteen minutes. Ron has an incredible sense of humor, the incense burned for over an hour. As the mist turned to rain and the rain turned to a downpour, they burned and scented our little spot. I had promised to stay until they went out, and later as I gathered my bucket, incense holders and spent wicks, I said, "I love you now as I did before and I will wear this new ring to honor that love. I will keep you next to me, even though you made me a drippy, cold and soggy mess. See you on the other side."

*

MARY POTTER KENYON
Mary's 60-year-old husband David
died of heart failure in 2012

People have often commented how blessed I am to have children at home, as I've handled the grief from the loss of my mother (2010), husband (2012), and grandson (2013), without understanding that it is specifically because I have children at home that I've felt the need to hide some of my grief. While they have seen me cry, I had to hide some of my own pain to help them through their own, particularly the loss of a father. Was it a good thing that I had to hold it all together to protect my children? Perhaps, but it also meant that I could not moan in sadness in the middle of the night because an eight year old had crawled into bed with me, and was right beside me.

When family members would comment, "You are doing so well," I occasionally took this as an affront, and read between the lines "You must not have loved him so much, as you seem fine." They had no idea how badly I really was doing. I was dropping the ball on so many things those first few months, and I still have not returned to being the mother I once was. Maybe I never will cook regular meals again, since my meals were planned for my husband. Maybe using the dryer, instead of hanging out my laundry is a transgression that can be forgiven. I do what I have to do to get through each day, and sometimes that means I am going to skip a family get-together because I can't bear seeing all the couples together. I feel as though I wear a heavy cloak of sadness, one that separates me from family and friends who cannot understand. It is there at all times, sometimes heavier than others. I don't think anyone but another widow would understand.

Don't forget us after the first year. I had a fairly good support system that first year, but it seemed like most people stopped asking how I was doing after that. Grief doesn't end at one year. Don't ever say "You need to get professional help." This is a judgment of my grieving. I was working two jobs and completely exhausted. It was natural to fall apart under tremendous stress. Being a single parent is hard. I would burst into tears when someone would ask how I was doing. Grief can come in waves. We might be fine one day, and falling apart the next. Just be there for us through the waves. Please don't tell us how to grieve. Until you have experienced the same thing, you actually cannot know how you will react. Everyone grieves in their own way.

*

NANCY REDMOND
Nancy's 40-year-old husband Kevin
died of a heart attack in 2012

My emotions make me feel very bipolar. In almost every instance in my life, my moods and emotions could swing between elation (such as at my daughter's wedding) and the raw pain of loss of my best friend. I also have a very difficult time making everyday decisions, such as what to have for dinner. Likewise, I also struggle with big life-altering decisions, such as whether to look for a new job or home. Read between the lines. When I say I'm okay, look into my eyes. You'll see the truth. Understand that I am still very confused about everything, and my decision-making skills have been affected. Never, ever hesitate to give advice. I promise I'll take it to heart, even if I don't follow your suggestion. I don't always make sense when I'm upset. I understand that more than you know, and I can't make sense of anything some days. I am also not rational when I am upset and believe me, I know that, too.

*

MARYELLEN ROACH
MaryEllen's sister Suzette and two nieces, 6-year-old
Vivian and 8-year-old Lillian, died in car accident in 2012

My emotions are like the ocean's tide, sometimes things are calm and other times it's a hurricane. After a loss, thousands of emotions are rolled into one word, and that word is grief. While dealing with grief, emotions become much less predictable and less controllable than they once were. Something may not upset me one day, but the next, it may instantly bring tears and a panic attack. Due to my emotionally inconsistent reactions, I try to shelter myself from things I feel might upset me. I also keep a lot of my deep emotions to myself as to not upset my family and friends. Be aware that we may not tell you the whole truth of how we're feeling. But don't push us to divulge all the thoughts or emotions we're having.

Be prepared to listen if we begin talking about our experience. Recognize that every grief is unique. Allow us to grieve in our own way, as long as we are not physically harming ourselves or anyone else.

*

MARY LEE ROBINSON
Mary Lee's 63-year-old husband Pat
died of a sudden cerebral hemorrhage in 2013

It took the telling and retelling and then telling some more, the story of my loss, especially when my husband died. I vomited my emotions to anyone who indicated a willingness to listen by merely looking at me. I had no discrimination at all. In time, I regained control and became more selective with whom I shared my thoughts. Dealing with a newly minted griever isn't pleasant work, but it's a karma thing. Someday, you will need someone to deal with you in your grief. Suck it up and listen. Be like the church pastor, like your Human Resources Officer. Treat the information, sometimes confessions, as sacred and classified information, not the fodder for gossip, because your turn is coming. Bear in mind, the more we are allowed to talk, the faster the healing will begin, and the less you'll be called upon to listen. Don't try to hand your griever off to another griever. The second griever is carrying enough of a burden; the first griever wants to talk to a friend, not some stranger who is a griever. As a friend, it's your job. You'll want your friends around you when your time comes. Invite the griever to join you in activities, including dinner with your family. Don't rope them off, thinking they only want to be alone. Sometimes that's true, but not always. If your griever isn't up to joining you for one occasion, don't stop asking. It shows that you care. It's a gesture you will appreciate too. Understand that you will have to do the heavy lifting of a friendship. The griever needs to be coddled for a longer while than your patience will last. Do it anyway. Consoling a griever is a terrible burden. There's a bigger burden: being the griever. At some point, you will be.

*

ALEXIS VON UTTER
Alexis was 12 when her father Marc
died at age 57 from lung cancer complications

Yes, I kept to myself and acted happy, I didn't want to be the freak who just lost her dad. I hated that everything was changed, and everyone just felt bad for me.

*

HEATHER WALLACE-REY
Heather was 40 when her father John
died suddenly at age 71 of a massive heart attack

I was very angry during much of the grieving process. I was angry with my dad for dying. I was angry at myself for not calling Dad when I should have, which meant I never got a chance to say "I love you" one more time. I was also very angry at God. Help us find an outlet. Whether it's exercise or writing or a hobby, doing something to "take the edge off" will really help.

*

DIANNE WEST
Dianne's 69-year-old husband Vern
died from multiple myeloma in 2010

There are so many triggers in those early days. A song, a memory, a photo, a smell. Or something as simple as picking up the mail and finding an envelope addressed to him. Tears are so close to the surface, and can spill so easily – but tears can be healing, so I let them fall. Don't turn away. Grab a tissue, and hug us as you hand it to us. And let us talk. Allow us to grieve the way we need; there are no rules. Let us be quiet; sometimes there are just no words.

*

CHAPTER NINE

UNDERSTANDING OUR REACTIONS

Do not apologize for crying. Without
this emotion, we are only robots.
ELIZABETH GILBERT

In the prior chapter we explored our emotions. In this chapter, we'll explore our reactions to the various questions we face by well-meaning people in the aftermath of our loss.

Certain questions can evoke predictable reactions, such as the sense of dread when a bereaved mother is asked how old her children are. As a result, many of us find solace in hibernating at home, safe from small talk that organically arises from a familiar face in the checkout line of the local grocery store. While that small talk might appear innocent to most, to the bereaved it can represent dangerous territory full of landmines.

If we could paint our sensitivities and resulting reactions onto a mural, it would look a bit like one enormous scribble. Scrawl after scrawl, in red and orange and yellow and pink and purple and black and blue. Sometimes we are able to temper our reactions and sometimes they come spewing uncontrollably. It's not right. It's not wrong. Sometimes it's not fair. But that is how sorrow is.

Please don't be afraid that you will open up wounds when you talk to us. The wounds are opened and we need trusted people to help us heal, as much as possible, in our own way. Know that losing a loved one drastically changes a person. Don't expect us to stay the same. Accept that.

In this chapter, as in the last, the writers offer valuable insight into the various journeys and reactions from which to learn.

Forget Me Nots

1. **We're predictably unpredictable.**
   Our emotions are predictably unpredictable; so are our reactions. Our reactions will mirror the emotions we're feeling at that moment.

2. **Emotional overloads can lead to reactive meltdowns.**
   Please be patient. A good night's sleep or a nap can help.

3. **Grief is exhausting.**
   Exhaustion makes us crabby. Help us reduce stressors.

4. **Don't take it personally.**
   Sometimes our emotional distress cause us to react in less than graceful ways.

5. **Don't be afraid.**
   Our wounds are already open. It's okay to talk about it. And it's okay for us to not be okay.

6. **Your cues count.**
   Expect guarded answers if your physical cues give away your hesitancy or discomfort.

7. **We don't have all the answers either.**
   Grief doesn't come with an instruction manual. We wish it did.

8. **We overreact often.**
   Already overwhelmed by our feelings, small issues can quickly feel insurmountable.

9. **Full of surprises.**
   We often lose our filters. Prepare for offhanded comments or responses.

10. **Have compassion.**
   When you point out that we're repeating ourselves or we can't remember details, it makes us feel worse.

Thoughtful Insight

*

EMILY BAIRD-LEVINE
Emily's 43-year-old brother Don
died from a heart attack in 2004

I figured out very quickly who could tolerate listening to me describe the loss of my brother and who couldn't. If someone I could trust asked me how I was or asked about my loss, I would give them a genuine and feeling-filled answer. If not, I would just say that I was fine, and move on to another subject that the person I was talking to could handle. Don't hesitate to ask the bereaved how they are doing. Please only do so if you are willing to listen to them and let them feel whatever they are feeling at the moment.

*

EMILY BARNHARDT
Emily's 20-year-old friend/roommate
Hannah died by suicide in 2014

Some people find comfort in talking about their loved one often, while others find that they cope better maintaining a boundary of privacy around their grief. When asked questions, factors like personality, the type of loss, and the relationship one had with their loved one will all influence the way the bereaved respond to questions from others. No response is better than another, so it's important for support people to observe and learn how the grieving individual feels and reacts to questions about their loved one and their loved one's death.

If you are trying to support someone through grief, and are unsure over how to approach something like this, it's appropriate to just simply ask the bereaved whether or not it's helpful to talk about their loved one. Let the bereaved person give you guidance on what is and isn't helpful for them, and ask if there are certain times or situations when they know they don't want to discuss their loss. When we are unsure of what's helpful, simply asking the grieving person will relieve us from that burdening feeling of walking on eggshells around them. It will also likely mean a lot to the bereaved to know that you want to learn how to support them.

Hannah died by suicide, and I wrestled a lot in my grief over how to respond when people asked me questions about her death. Suicide is, unfortunately, a taboo subject shrouded with stigma, so grievers who've lost someone to suicide will often have a diverse range of reactions, even just to questions. I noticed an air of awkwardness and avoidance in many conversations when I mentioned Hannah, and the feeling that she, herself, had become a taboo subject broke my heart. Regardless, I personally chose to be honest when people asked questions about how Hannah passed or what happened; I didn't want to feel like I had to hide the truth. I also found comfort in talking about her, so I appreciated people asking me questions about the person she was. I was often afraid to be the one to bring her up or talk about what happened; I was worried I would annoy people or push them away if I talked about it too much. I didn't want to burden people, and I feared that they secretly might not want to talk about it to begin with. I often felt relief when people mentioned her or asked how I was doing.

I didn't always feel relief, however. I responded differently to questions from others, based on who was asking and what their intentions were. For example, I remember meeting with a woman who worked in the office at my college to talk about resources that might help me during my grief. Upon hearing that Hannah died by suicide, the focus of the conversation dramatically shifted. I could feel this woman's curiosity burning as she suddenly started asking questions. "How did she do it?" "Did you see it coming?" "Did you find her?" "Did she leave a note?" I remember being taken aback and bothered by her intrusive curiosity. She'd only known me for about fifteen minutes, and she certainly didn't know Hannah. She wasn't a counselor, and her questions weren't serving to help me, so it wasn't her business to ask something so personal. It's never appropriate to pry, and a grieving person is often quite aware of peoples' intentions.

For me, the type of questions that were helpful were ones from trusted people and ones who served to give me an opportunity to open up if I wanted to. Those types of questions demonstrated to me that they cared and wanted to know, if I wanted to share. That meant a great deal to me. To address the issue of suicide and how this type of loss might affect a person's hesitation to answer questions about how their loved one died, I can only speak to my own experience, as it's different for everyone.

For me, there were often feelings of anxiety when I answered questions. Hannah and I lived together; she was my family. I ached deeply with guilt that someone as close to me as family could be in that much pain without me being aware and knowing the seriousness of it.

Therefore, when I answer peoples' questions sometimes, I can't help but wonder what that person is thinking about me: Was I a bad friend to Hannah? Did I love her well, or was I selfish and oblivious to her pain? How could I have let it happen? Did I know? Did I even try to help her? In reality, I have no idea if these thoughts ever actually cross anyone's mind and I think my insecurity over it shows me that I honestly still wrestle with those questions myself sometimes.

Many people feel hesitant to even share that a loved one died by suicide because of the stigma around it and because of these exact types of question that might go through peoples' minds. Keep this in mind as you support someone grieving a loss by suicide. They may be wrestling with questions like these. You can help by honoring their loved one and offering gentle encouragement and validation of their love for the deceased.

*

ERICA GALE BELTZ
Erica's 5-year-old son Luke Jordan died in 2002
from a fallen banister in his aunt's driveway

The hardest time for me in the beginning was the morning. Even before I knew I was awake yet, I would open my eyes, and there seemed to be this incredible space. First darkness and silence. Then I would hear the sounds of morning or see a glimpse of daylight coming through the blinds. It was as if I wasn't even in my own body, kind of like I was watching myself wake up from across the room. There would be confusion or, if I was awake, then more confusion as to whether I was even alive. Once I realized it wasn't just a horrible nightmare, pain would fill every ounce of me, and the devastation would set in again. I needed to be strong for my daughter but couldn't find the strength or the courage. I wanted to hide from the rest of the world. The pain was dark, consuming and unbearable. I missed out on a young nephew growing up because it just hurt to get close to a little boy.

*

SOPHIA BLOWERS
Sophia was 50 when her mother Amy
died at age 79 of internal bleeding

My reaction was based upon whether someone was just polite, or because they wanted to carry part of my burden. I would often have "canned" answers: I am fine. She is in a better place. It was a peaceful passing. The family is closer than ever. Many of these answers were bald-faced lies, but they protected me from those asking insincerely and protected others who were asking just to be kind. The few people I trust with my soul got the real answers: Today is hard. I miss her. I am having nightmares. My siblings are tearing each other to pieces. You learn to discern those you can open up to and those you can't. And for some, there are just those who "get" you and will hold you up.

*

LYNDA CHELDELIN FELL
Lynda's 15-year-old daughter Aly
died in a car accident in 2009

The truth is that I dreaded going out in public because, inevitably, Aly came up. As predicted, once I shared she had passed away, the looks of pity started and the conversation ended. I understood. I am and will always be, "that" mother, the one who lost her child. Once a grieving mother, always a grieving mother. It was a lifelong sentence with no chance for parole.

At first, I desperately wanted to talk about Aly to anyone who would listen to me ramble, but it made others so uncomfortable that I learned to keep my cards close to my heart. I pretended to be okay, because I desperately wanted to feel normal, even if my heart told me I would never be normal again. If I could convince others, perhaps I would begin to believe it myself, right? Now that I'm active in the bereavement field, I realize the err of my way. By pretending I was okay, I gave the impression that I was "healed" of my broken heart, just like neighbor Joe's broken arm or Aunt Suzie's heartburn.

Recently I was honored as the Camp Fire organization's 2015 inspirational speaker, which shocked me because bereaved mothers usually aren't the first in line when one comes looking for inspiration. I wasn't nervous about being on the podium; I had done that many times before. But this time my audience was different; they weren't the bereaved. So sharing my story about Aly for the purpose of inspiring a different audience was a new twist. I fully expected to lose some audience members to bathroom breaks or "needing to make a phone call," as some just can't bear such a heavy topic. But as I shared my story and my heart, not one person moved. And when I finished, I was given a standing ovation. I burst into tears on the podium out of sheer gratitude that not only had the audience not run from my story, they embraced it. I was so used to being "that" mother, the one people avoided because I had lost a child, that I cried for the next three days from the sheer emotion of that standing ovation. For the rest of my life, I believe that audience will never know what that meant to my broken heart. Never again will I avoid questions about my daughter. If my story somehow inspires others, that's a silver lining I treasure.

*

MICHELLE DETWILER
Michelle's 19-year-old daughter Emily
died in 2014 due to congenital complications

When asked how I was feeling, there were some people I just couldn't answer truthfully. I didn't know them well enough to really tell them how I felt. Often times, I didn't say much. How could I tell an acquaintance that I'm not happy? Would they think I was crazy? I remember one thing that happened that made me feel like I was dying inside. At the end of the school year, I saw pictures of my daughter's peers on social media at their graduation parties. They were nice family pictures, wearing their cap and gown, doing special things because they were the graduate. My child would have graduated with them. I was angry that her peers and their families were having such fun. My child was gone, and we missed her so much! Those to whom I confessed my anger to this situation were able to be patient with me. How wonderful that they listened. I don't know if they understood my reaction to the graduates and their families, but they listened without judgment.

It's important to never take for granted how we're going to react. Listen and accept our feelings. Even though our emotions may not seem rational, they feel very real to us. There might not be a "fix" for the emotions or reactions. Know that tomorrow is a new day, and feelings often change after a night's sleep. Sometimes it's helpful to suggest we take a break or remove ourselves from the situation at hand.

*

CHRISTINE DUMINIAK
Christine's 86-year-old mother Ann
died from an aortic aneurysm in 2004

I never minded questions from others, because it gave me an opportunity to share some amazing spiritual experiences I had with my parents, which gave me a great deal of joy. In looking back, I do not regret anything that I did during the grief process, and would do everything the same way.

*

SHARON EHLERS
Sharon's best friend Joy died in 2009 at age 52
Sharon's former fiancé John died in 2012 at age 59

When someone asks about how either Joy or John died I have always answered with the truth. They committed suicide. It's been my experience that very few people want to know the dreaded "how" so I never say it unless they ask. For the very few (and there haven't been many) who are interested (or morbidly curious) I give them high level details. Most people can't deal with suicide, so I had to find a way to deal with it myself. That's why I sought out the Survivors After Suicide support group. Talking about it there gave me the comfort and support I needed. There was no stigma, no funny looks, no one changing the subject.

*

ANNAH ELIZABETH
Annah's newborn son Gavin Michael
died 26 minutes following his birth

This response is also as layered as the onion. In the earliest months following my son's birth, I often found myself face to face with people who hadn't heard about his death. One of the first questions they would ask is, "How's the baby?" The excitement and enthusiasm on their faces would turn to shock and fear when I responded, "I'm sorry; he didn't make it." That was the only answer I could summon and was the one I continued to provide for that query.

Once I had children in tow, the questions changed. "Is this your first?" and "How many children do you have?" were the most common. My answer often depended on things like how much time I had, how much energy I had, and the context of the conversation. Sometimes I'd talk about Gavin, and sometimes I'd just reply by providing the count of my living children. It was often just easier to respond with the latter.

But as time went on and I began doing more and more work on the healing side of grief, I realized it didn't have to be all or nothing, and I wanted to find ways to be honest about my experiences and to honor those children who are now only with me in spirit.

You can usually tell if someone is engaged or just being polite by how closely they are paying attention. If someone asks a question like, "What's he studying?" then you know they are truly interested. Once I share stories of the three youngest children, I will usually say something like, "My eldest is here with us in spirit; he died shortly after birth," or if I've gleaned that the person has a sense of humor and understands that parenting isn't all pride and perfection, I might respond with, "My eldest died shortly after birth; he's here with us in spirit and wreaking havoc in Heaven."

It is almost inevitable that if the conversation goes that far, the other person will begin sharing their loss experiences or the experiences of someone they know. The miscarriages always come into those conversations and I am continually amazed and inspired by the number of people who say to me, "I had a miscarriage twenty years ago; it's something we don't talk about," or "My sister/aunt/mother/friend/neighbor had a miscarriage and she's never recovered."

*

BRENDA KLEINSASSER
Brenda's 88 year-old mother
died from congestive heart failure in 2011

Some days are still difficult. There are still very few people who I can share that with. Don't expect me to be open all of the time about my loss. It will take time for me to gauge who I can or cannot trust to share deep feelings with. Don't get angry. We are trying to figure out each day how we will continue to cope with our loss. We are not upset with you. We are trying to find our own way to deal with this.

*

DEANA MARTIN
Deana's only two children, 25-year-old Amanda
and 21-year-old Logan, died in a car accident in 2011

Each day is still a challenge. In the beginning, I don't know how I made it. To know that each moment another person feels the immense pain of grief brings me great sadness. There is so much I want to share with the world about this journey and how to help those in the dark recesses of grief. Grief of this magnitude has been the hardest thing I have ever faced, and I am passionate about making the road easier for others, even if just a little. Don't avoid us, this just leaves us more isolated. Don't be afraid to bring up our loved one. We cherish the opportunity to speak of our loved ones. Say their name. Remember that we are suffering an intense psychological injury. We can no more pick up and go on as a man who lost his arm in an accident can grow a new one.

*

DIANE MCKENZIE-SAPP
Diane's 65-year-old husband Ron
died from renal failure in 2006

I think differently from most people. I think and dream in Technicolor images. I began to dream of a widow's ring almost immediately after Ron's death. I prayed for help: to sleep, to stop hurting, to stop crying, and to move away from the grayness. My dreams were of rings, wedding bands, mourning rings, and rings I had never seen before. When I woke, it became necessary for me to draw those new rings. I grew to understand that these visions were the help I had prayed for. The rings were for widows! What? Why? Did someone upstairs think that an insignificant widow could change the plight of widows around the world with a ring? Impossible. When I returned to work, my coworkers would avoid me. Their offhand question of "How are you doing?" was met with "I am designing a widow's ring," and the look of "she has finally lost her mind" would come over their faces. I explained that I was making a widow's ring because I felt invisible. They would reply, "I never heard of that," meaning that if it hasn't been invented by now, it has to be senseless.

The idea of a widow's ring was refused on every level. I was a naïve fool to the jeweler's world, rebuffed and refused. *Shark Tank*, the home shopping networks, and the small and large jewelry stores each could not see a profit for them, and were unwilling to try anything different. Their bottom line did not include whimsy for the widows. The widow was crushed but the little girl who lives inside once again said, "Why not?" The concept, although unusual, was worthy; actually it was a godsend. My dreams were visions of rings, and I was compelled to draw them immediately in the morning. Back then, I did not understand how something so small could make me feel better. I did not know how it would anchor me, and hold a connection to all that I held dear. I read that it was Queen Victoria who had the first concept of mourning jewelry. No one was allowed to come to court unless they wore black clothing and black jewelry to honor the memory of her spouse. I would do no less for my spouse.

During the Civil War, Americans followed the same custom. Queen Victoria's edict remained in effect for over two decades. There are lovely examples of mourning jewelry in museums, and their color and design played heavily into my contemporary mourning jewelry designs. The age of mourning jewelry ended with Queen Victoria's death. This concept has to live on past me, and I worry that it won't. I have not completely figured this out. God helps those who help themselves, and He had provided so far. He puts exactly the right person in my path exactly at the right time. I must pass it forward. He has sent windfalls each time I said, "I give up." And he has put my cancer in remission so I can finish the last designs. He will prevail. It may be a part of God's plan. But I did have two questions for God. "Did you have to take my husband and my mother and father for me to truly understand the pain of grief? When you told Noah to build that boat, did YOU give him any plans, and more importantly, did you give him any money to make it happen?" I am still alive so I guess he is not annoyed.

*

JULIE MJELVE
Julie's 42-year-old husband Cameron
died by suicide in 2011

It was difficult for me to talk about my husband's death initially. Sometimes I simply couldn't talk about it, other times I only half answered the questions. One thing I did to help handle questions from others was to create my own mourning symbol. I wasn't ready to take my wedding ring off, but I wasn't ready for people to ask where my husband was. So I tied a black ribbon around my wedding ring as a way of hopefully getting people to notice that something was different and that they should hopefully think about it before they started asking questions. As time went on, I was able to answer more of the questions, or provide more details. Now, I can even let people know the information they might need sometimes before they ask the question. Looking back, I don't think I would have done anything differently. I think it's important for others to know that you can't always hold it together when you are grieving, and they should not expect you to. It's okay to be sad, and we shouldn't have to feel uncomfortable about being sad when a loved one has passed away.

*

MARY POTTER KENYON
Mary's 60-year-old husband David
died of heart failure in 2012

I love talking about the people I have lost; it keeps them alive in our memories. Not a day goes by that my youngest daughters and I don't mention their dad. I hear, "I miss Dad" daily. And I reply, "Me, too. But that's a good thing. He deserves to be missed and loved." As for other family members and friends, they have moved on with their lives. If they take the time to ask me how I am doing, I hesitate. Do they really want to know that I still cry at least once a day? Sometimes only a sob or two, or a few tears at the grocery store when I see a woman pushing her husband in a wheelchair, or a couple holding hands. People who love us want us to be okay. I don't think they really want to hear the truth; that we are having a difficult time. I think I need to be more open with my answers. My husband always advised that I just "tell the truth," and since his death I've tried to follow that advice. "It is just too hard," I've said when someone asks why I don't always go to church, or why I miss a family event. There are very few people I can be totally open and honest with. I get the feeling most people would rather not hear about loss or grief, and I understand that. However, it helps me to be able to talk about my husband and grandson, to say their names. I carry some anger in me for those who profess to care about me aren't asking important questions, or checking to see if I am okay.

*

NANCY REDMOND
Nancy's 40-year-old husband Kevin
died of a heart attack in 2012

I became angry when I unfairly expected people to know what I needed. I understand now how unreasonable it was to expect someone who wasn't in the ever-swirling "snow globe" with me to somehow magically say or do that one thing that would make everything better. I regret those days when I was crabby or lashed out at the loving souls who mean the most to me in this world. Grief didn't come with an instruction manual for me, or for them.

Don't ask me questions that I don't know the answer to. It makes me frustrated to say "I don't know" all the time. Don't take my frustration or seemingly angry attitude as lashing out against those around me. Don't make decisions for me, even though you think they are right. Everything is out of my control, and please, please, please allow me to decide on the things that *are* within my control. Don't take away my "securities." If I have always hosted Christmas Eve dinner, please don't change things up on me. I need "constants" in my life to carry on. Things won't always be this way, and I am certain that given some time, I will be much less regimented and unbending. Just understand right now that things need to stay the same as much as they possibly can.

*

MARYELLEN ROACH
MaryEllen's sister Suzette and two nieces, 6-year-old
Vivian and 8-year-old Lillian, died in car accident in 2012

Only a couple of my friends receive truly honest answers when they ask how I'm doing. I have found it difficult to be honest because truthful answers upset my friends, which is more upsetting to me. Sometimes their distress even makes me angry, because how can they possibly expect an honest answer after I lost half my family? I've found that sharing my raw feelings with fellow members in support groups helps me more, because they aren't emotionally attached to me. Since they don't know me other than in the support group, they only offer support without becoming upset about my unhappiness. We are typically overwhelmed by our feelings, and cannot always handle other issues. Sometimes that leads to an overreaction to a small problem or something that isn't a problem at all. Try not to take a negative reaction personally.

Don't be offended if we don't share our true feelings with you. Sometimes it's easier to just not talk about it. Our emotions can change second to second and day to day, so do our reactions.

*

MARY LEE ROBINSON
Mary Lee's 63-year-old husband Pat
died of a sudden cerebral hemorrhage in 2013

Particularly in the beginning, but even now I get a lot of people who try and "should on me." They'll make statements like, "I think you should.....fill in the blank." Whether it is sell the extra car, sell the house, don't sell the house, get a job, don't get a job, take your rings off, start dating, don't date, etc. All of these pearls of wisdom are unsolicited, unasked for, unwelcome. All served not to "fix" me, but throw anger and resentment into the complex mixed cocktail of emotions with which I wrestled. I lost some decades long as well as some shorter friendships.

Ask! Ask yourself why you are asking? Is it a matter that's pivotal to the griever's safety and well-being? Or are you just meddling? What's your stake in your question? Don't judge! My needs and decisions are not the same as yours, and not the same as what mine used to be. I know you think you know what you would do. I assure you, until it's happened to you, you have no inkling.

*

HEATHER WALLACE-REY
Heather was 40 when her father John
died suddenly at age 71 of a massive heart attack

My reactions to everyday life, to statements, and to questions that people had really varied right after Dad died. My husband knew every detail of how I was feeling, as did my best friend and my closest friends. For the most part, however, I was a "loose cannon" as far as how I would react to any given situation or question that people asked about Dad. Understand that we go

148

through a hurricane of emotions. Understand that we aren't always in a good place to answer questions, and respect our need for time to find the right words.

*

DIANNE WEST
Dianne's 69-year-old husband Vern
died from multiple myeloma in 2010

Most of the time, I was not honest in my responses to questions or statements. I would say, "I'm doing okay" or "thank you," and then ask them a question. That always changed the focus, and they would go on and on about themselves, and I could just nod in support. I didn't feel they really wanted to hear how bad things were, so it was easier to just not share the truth of how hard this was. Be cautious about asking detailed questions about the loss as that can feel intrusive. Our person is dead; the details of how they died are personal, unless we choose to share them. You may see a change in our personality; accept it with love. Yes, I was strong during those cancer/caregiving years, but hearing you say that now that he's gone is not at all comforting. We often lose our filters after a loss, and you may be surprised by an out-of-character comment or response. Let it pass.

*

We're calm on the surface
but . . . .

CHAPTER TEN

UNDERSTANDING OUR COMFORT

We all lose somebody we care about and want to find some comforting way of dealing with it, something that will give us a little closure, a little peace.

MITCH ALBOM

When we lose someone we love, no matter how prepared we think we are for the journey, it quite simply isn't enough. We are left standing at the starting gate suddenly unsure of when, where, and exactly how to take that first step. Although thousands have trekked this very path before, we feel inadequate, isolated and woefully unprepared. Where will the journey take us, and what do we need along the way? Everything in loss is unpredictable, including our comfort. What feels comforting today might feel irritating tomorrow. Like most of the grief journey, there is no rhyme or reason to the ways we seek and find comfort along the way. As our support, you are a big part of our survival pack. You can offer things that bring us comfort, guide us, and illuminate the journey so it doesn't feel quite as lonely.

Do you know where we can get this fixed?

Our Comfort

Holding a loved one's possession.
Their favorite watch, stuffed animal or other treasured possession allows us to feel close to our loved one when it's in our hands.

Wearing their clothes and accessories.
Our loved one's bathrobe, slippers, jewelry, T-shirts, socks and sweatpants are common clothing that brings us comfort. Some of us find it helpful to have our loved one's clothing made into a quilt or pillow we can snuggle with.

Filling the void.
Holding onto a pillow can be very soothing when our arms feel empty. Consider buying a special pillow that fits perfectly in our arms, or is extra soft and in our loved one's favorite color.

Personalize it.
Gifts adorning our loved one's name or photo brings comfort to most, and becomes a treasured keepsake we'll cherish. Consider a Christmas tree ornament or a locket containing our loved one's photo, a photo album embroidered with their name, a picture frame or bracelet engraved with their name, or a locket containing a photo of our loved one's thumbprint.

Books & Audio
Bereavement books reassure us that others have survived the journey. Meditation tapes soothe the rawness. Inspirational books lift the heart. A CD with our loved one's favorite songs can bring great comfort too.

We yearn for familiarity.
Eating our loved one's favorite food, watching their favorite movie, and going through photos, sports memorabilia, or our loved one's artwork can bring great comfort. Gathering their photos, certificates, and momentos to create scrapbooks or photo albums can be soothing.

Connecting.

Connecting with others either by volunteering at a homeless shelter or connecting with bereavement groups who have experienced a similar loss is very comforting, as it reminds us that we aren't alone. Those who are ahead on the journey give us hope that the journey is survivable.

Expressive writing.

Penning our thoughts using a journal, spiral notebook, or diary allows us to vent our emotions in a safe environment away from judgment or scrutiny. This is also useful for those who fear they'll forget the little things. Writing them down gives us a place to safely store our memories and ease the fear of forgetting moments we treasured.

Silence.

Stillness, quietness, and meditation can help us feel safe and grounded.

Aromatherapy.

Essential and fragrance oils have proven to lift or calm our mood, increase cognitive function and reduce anxiety. Consider soothing candles, diffusers, jewelry diffusers, luxury soap, bath salts, bath oils, potpourris, etc.

Miracle of music.

Whether we enjoy listening to our loved one's favorite songs, or tranquil nature sounds, music has been shown to have ability to help organize the brain and elevate the mood.

Our pets.

Interaction with our pets has been scientifically proven to reduce anxiety and lift our spirits. It also offers a safe, nonjudgmental form of socializing.

Gift of Comedy.

It's been said that one laugh scatters a hundred griefs. While death and comedy don't seem like a good pairing, comedic therapy is a good way to get out of our own heads for thirty minutes. A healthy dose of laughter can provide an emotional release that deserves recognition.

Forget Me Nots

1. **Remember the memory.**
   Memory problems are common after loss. Patience is key when we repeat ourselves or forget things.

2. **We're overwhelmed.**
   Sometimes too overwhelmed to ask for help.

3. **We still need to cry.**
   It's a good sign that we're processing the loss.

4. **No act is too small.**
   Kindness comes in all sizes and shapes.

5. **Think outside the box.**
   What do you think we might need?

6. **No rhyme or reason.**
   What brings comfort one day, such as looking at pictures or rereading Facebook messages, might bring pain the next.

7. **Light the way.**
   Help us find ways to let the sunshine in.

8. **Reassurance.**
   We just lost someone we deeply love, along with our familiarity of the world as we knew it. In the face of such an unfamiliar future, we need reassurance that you won't leave us too.

9. **Compassion.**
   Don't direct us. Walk with us.

10. **Patience.**
    We may be weepy, irritable and clingy....in the same moment.

11. Something to hold.
Tangible items help us feel connected with our loved one.

12. Be our wingman.
As we seek to find our own comfort, just go with the flow and allow our instincts to guide us. We might find it where we least expect it.

Thoughtful Insight

*

EMILY BARNHARDT
Emily's 20-year-old friend/roommate
Hannah died by suicide in 2014

I think when it comes to knowing which items would be most helpful for your loved one grieving, it comes down to knowing who they are as a person and if they have any unique needs at that moment. Meals are always helpful, I think. I personally had no appetite for a while after Hannah passed, but I know meals might have been helpful for me in those moments I did. It really depends on the person. Are there daily things that person needs? If so, that might be an area in which a support person could help. Do they have children they need to regularly get supplies for caretaking purposes?

When it comes to helpful items, I think it's unique to each grieving person. Ask if you are unsure, but keep in mind that a grieving person might feel too overwhelmed or too guilty to ask for something. So if you're certain there is an immediate need during the initial aftermath of the loss that you know you can meet, go ahead and do it. There is no helpful act that is too small in the aftermath of a loss. I can assure you it will be noticed, and most likely, it will be greatly appreciated.

We are often too overwhelmed or could feel too guilty to ask for help. Household tasks, errands, meals, etc. Anything that will help us feel less alone and that will remind us of how loved we are. Handwritten cards or notes are heartfelt and touching, and it demonstrates a person's love for us in taking the time to do that.

*

CHRISTINE BASTONE
Christine's sister Elizabeth
died in 2012 at age 38

I find that touching pictures of Liz comforts me. Holding a teddy bear, a 1973 penny (1973 is the year Liz was born), or for some reason, a little blue or clear accent gem (I call them stones, and got them at The Dollar Tree) is comforting for me. Since Liz's favorite color was blue, almost anything blue can comfort me too. Find out what year our loved one was born, and then try to find a penny with that year on it for us. Offer something in our loved one's favorite color. Offer a personal or personalized gift of some sort: a Christmas tree ornament, a necklace or a bracelet, a photo album or picture frame. Put our loved one's name on the ornament, engrave the jewelry or put pictures in the album or frame.

*

ERICA GALE BELTZ
Erica's 5-year-old son Luke Jordan died in 2002
from a fallen banister in his aunt's driveway

We must have played the DVD from the funeral home a thousand times. We made CDs with Luke's favorite music, and played them over and over. We played home movies countless times so we could hear his voice. We went through every box and drawer in search for any trace of Luke's life. I loved all the things that people made in his memory. I kept his favorite treasures within reach. I also slept with his pajamas and jacket for as long as I can remember. If you see something that makes you smile because it evokes a memory of our loved one, buy it for us and share the memory.

*

SOPHIA BLOWERS
Sophia was 50 when her mother Amy
died at age 79 of internal bleeding

My mom's watch was the thing I held onto. She wore that watch every day. It was her signature to always have a watch on. When she died, I held on to her bathrobe, slippers and watch. The things that brought her the most comfort and were the most important to her are the things that matter most to me.

*

LYNDA CHELDELIN FELL
Lynda's 15-year-old daughter Aly
died in a car accident in 2009

Someone gave each of us a blue heart-shaped stone to carry in our pocket. Aly's favorite color was blue, and the heart represented her love. While out doing errands, I often put my hand in my pocket just to feel the cool, smooth stone and it comforted me to know my husband and children were doing the same. We carried those stones in our pockets for years.

*

MICHELLE DETWILER
Michelle's 19-year-old daughter Emily
died in 2014 due to congenital complications

Our daughter, Emily, loved trucks, the large kind, trailer trucks. When they would drive down the road we would say, "Look Emily, here comes a red truck!" I found that even after her death, I often would say to myself, "Oh look! There's a red truck!" To this day, it continues to make me feel good to notice things that she liked. After Emily's death I missed hugging her and smelling her hair. For months I hugged and smelled her stuffed Piglet (from *Winnie the Pooh* stories). She had lots of "kids," but Piglet was her favorite. Often we would place Piglet next to her when she went to sleep, and I would come in to check on her, and Piglet would be on her chest or on her neck sleeping with her. This always amazed me because our daughter could not move her arms in a purposeful way. How did Piglet get up there? She was a tricky girl sometimes! Emily wore ponytails or a long braid almost every day. She had some very fancy pony bands with ribbons and sparkles on them. I took those bands and wore them on my wrist like a bracelet. This was my favorite "feeling close to her" thing that I did after she died. Also, her clothes are still in her dresser. In those first days, I would go through my daughter's dresser feeling her clothes and hug them, imagining her in it. I used up the rest of my daughter's remaining shampoo so I could still smell her. Although most of my daughter's clothing didn't fit me, I confiscated and wore all of my daughter's socks that fit me.

*

SHARON EHLERS
Sharon's best friend Joy died in 2009 at age 52
Sharon's former fiancé John died in 2012 at age 59

Talking to other people about both Joy and John also brings great comfort. Society has conditioned us not to open up or really talk about those who have died, especially if they died from suicide. I like to share personal memories and funny stories with people who did or didn't know them. Talking about them brings me peace. After Joy died, I wore her Guardian Angel bracelet. I had given it to her as a gift and, after she died, her husband agreed I could have it. I wore it all the time. It made me feel like a piece of her was with me. After John died, it was a little tougher. We had broken up, so I didn't have a lot of his personal possessions around. Household possessions just aren't the same. In those first few days I searched for things that were tangible reminders of him. I would even go into the men's cologne aisle so I could smell the cologne he used to wear. I am sure people thought I was crazy. Maybe more importantly, I began to think that I was crazy for doing that. I just felt desperate for something familiar.

*

ANNAH ELIZABETH
Annah's newborn son Gavin Michael
died 26 minutes following his birth

Some of the most precious items I have are the items that my nurses assembled for me. The littlest things like the bassinet card, my son's birth blanket and knitted cap, the paper measuring tape used to record his length, and the few instant photos they thought to take of my son wrapped in that blanket. Since my son died before I was able to bring him home, I was grateful that everything in the nursery was left just as I'd prepared it. Though those things also brought painful memories, they gave me many more hours of comfort in the weeks, months, and early years following his death.

*

DAPHNE GREER
Daphne's 5-year-old daughter Lydia
died in a car accident in 2008

After my daughter died, I lost all interest, control and hope in my life. Living in a constant daze, I considered it something to celebrate when I could actually get off the couch and retrieve my own drink of water. In the beginning, every step was a struggle, and I even had to consciously retrain myself to breath. Cooking, laundry, running errands and paying bills were chores I could not even begin to think about. Sleep was rare, and exhaustion was the normal. So comfort was scarce during the first few months after Lydia passed away. Nothing could comfort the excruciating pain I was experiencing. However, one thing that touched my heart was that another mother from my daughter's dance class came over to our house to just sit with me days after my daughter died. No words were said, just a loving embrace as she sat next to me holding my hand on the couch, for what seemed like endless hours. Her presence said everything. A couple of years later, I was at the carousel Lydia used to love to ride, and found the exact stuffed animal zebra that she adored hidden on the shelves. Instantly, I was overjoyed and bought it without hesitation. Having that connection (as we laid her worn and loved zebra to rest with her) means so much. This stuffed zebra has given me comfort many times when I needed it the most. Many things have warmed my heart, including God. He was my only reliable source of comfort. Also, seeing Lydia's artwork and pictures hanging in the house, hearing stories from others about my daughter, wearing my necklace made from her thumbprint and connecting with others who had experienced a similar loss.

*

BRENDA KLEINSASSER
Brenda's 88 year-old mother
died from congestive heart failure in 2011

My mother would sometimes rub my back when I would sit on the edge of her bed at the nursing home. She was trying to comfort me, as she knew this was difficult to be separated so much. I always think back to the conversation that we had in the nursing home about my promise to her. Mine was to live my life, and hers was always to remain in my heart. Whenever I would see something representing that promise, it would instantly give me comfort. I had a bracelet handcrafted that represents that promise. It is called "Transitions." It has two roses, which represent my mother, and a butterfly, which represents me coming into my own. When I see a butterfly, I think of that promise, and that truly gives me great comfort.

*

DEANA MARTIN
Deana's only two children, 25-year-old Amanda
and 21-year-old Logan, died in a car accident in 2011

Hospice was kind enough to make teddy bears from my children's robes, and I had a quilt made from their clothes. I find these items very helpful on the tough days. I remember one person brought me a grief book called *Roses in December*, and another friend brought me a coffee mug that said "hakuna matata" ("no worries") from *The Lion King*, which was my son's favorite movie. The book, *Roses in December*, was the first of many on healing from grief that I read, and I began a quest to read all I could find. Every time I open the cupboard and see the coffee cup, I smile and think to myself that my children are telling me, "No worries, Mom." I loved wearing their clothes in the beginning; it brought me comfort. When I would receive signs from them, was an incredible feeling, for then I knew they truly lived on. Writing was a big comfort to me, as well.

*

DIANE MCKENZIE-SAPP
Diane's 65-year-old husband Ron
died from renal failure in 2006

Before Ron passed away, I slept on my side and touched him with my back every night. I bought an extra long pillow that I would snuggle with, and the feeling of "something" behind me gave me a small measure of comfort. I used his pillow for my head and my pillow between my legs. I did not buy new sheets and rearrange the bedroom, as I have heard so many widows do. I tend to add things for comfort, and don't lean toward getting rid of things, but that is me, and I am a bit of a nut and a freewill hoarder. I also had a handkerchief to hold my tears (do not wash). Once you give your tears a place to rest and respect them, they will not be as relentless.

Hematite rings can be found inexpensively in several places and it was an excellent widow's ring. It is black, organic, and is said to absorb grief. I started selling them for this reason. After I wore the hematite for about three days, I was finally able to fall asleep and rest. I could tell I had rested because my hair, ears, and pillow were not wet from the tears that came whenever I laid down. I gave my father a hematite ring when Mom passed, and he wore it until the day he died. Hematite will shatter when it has absorbed as much grief as it can hold. To use for sleep or rest, the hematite does not have to be a ring, but it does have to be in contact with the skin. Bracelets and necklaces and rosary beads also work.

I sought other widows on the internet so I could belong somewhere. Being so absolutely alone is demoralizing, and I felt like I no longer belonged anywhere. I found solace in those groups. I lost myself for a while because it helped me "not be." I did not want to be in reality; Alice had her Wonderland, I had my Computerland. Checking-out was not an effective way to deal with grief. Each of us has to find our own path, and sometimes getting lost is part of that journey. Peer groups and other people in the same boat is a good thing. But don't think anyone in your boat has a clue about how to steer this ship. It is a godsend when you can see others who have piloted their ship to a safe harbor. Learn from them, and head in their direction, but always navigate and plot your own course.

*

JULIE MJELVE
Julie's 42-year-old husband Cameron
died by suicide in 2011

Meals were a big help in the initial aftermath. Something else that a friend initiated was a gift card to Starbucks. It offered me a moment to take a breather and step away emotionally a little bit from all that was going on, plus a moment to not have to worry about the finances of such a treat when there was so much focus on paying for the funeral and the aftermath. I have come to treasure those moments. I also received gift cards to places such as Wal-Mart or Save-On-Foods. Again, these were invaluable, as they helped to relieve some of the initial pressure on finances. I was able to use them to get groceries or clothes for the kids.

One of the greatest items I received from others was their time. People arranged babysitting for me so that I could take care of packing and selling our house. One lady, whom I will never forget, instead of offering a meal, took it one step further, and offered to take my grocery list. I, of course, declined, but she gently pushed, and I was so glad that she did. My children were so young (three years old, two years old and five months old) that constantly leaving them with babysitters to take care of everything was becoming very hard on them. So having the opportunity to stay home with them, and having my exact groceries essentially just appear was an absolute blessing. She also was in the position to pay for them - again, another incredible gift in a time when there were so many other financial changes with the loss of my husband's income, as well as the added pressures of funeral costs.

Finally, in coordination with the given item of "time and service," I was also given by some people the removal of judgment over the state of my home (housekeeping was not a top priority!), the choices I made in how to help myself as well as my children grieve, and the choices I made to help us all survive the upcoming days, months and years. Not everyone was able to give this gift; there were a lot of careless, not-thought-out words. But for a few, they were able to just simply come and give of their time and abilities. This item continues to be incredibly important to me, even four years later.

*

MARY POTTER KENYON
Mary's 60-year-old husband David
died of heart failure in 2012

For several months after my husband's death, I hugged one of his shirts as I fell asleep. I wore his watch around my wrist. It helped to have something tangible to hang onto.

As a writer, I found comfort in journaling, blogging, and writing essays about my loved ones. It was as if my words could keep them with me in some way. Pieces of my journal and blog ended up in a published book, *Refined By Fire: A Journey of Grief and Grace* (Familius, October 2014). I also read every book I could get my hands on about grief. It helped to read the stories of those who had been down this path of grief before me, knowing they had survived, and sometimes thrived after loss. I studied grief and the science of bereavement in order to understand it. I'd never held a study Bible until after my husband died, and wasn't sure how to find words of comfort in one, so I began a Bible study group. I found comfort in reading the Bible.

*

NANCY REDMOND
Nancy's 40-year-old husband Kevin
died of a heart attack in 2012

Sleeping in Kevin's clothing gave me comfort at night as did writing in my journal my deepest thoughts and pain. Activities that involved being with those I loved most in the world got me through the first hard days. To this day, being included in activities that also once included my husband gives me comfort. Talking about Kevin has always made my heart much more peaceful, as has wearing his shirts or his wedding band. I also wear his sweatshirt that says "Redmond" on it. Other things that bring me comfort include carrying his driver's license in my wallet and wearing his wedding ring. When I look at it, I am reminded that his wedding ring, which was on his finger the moment he passed to Heaven, was the only thing with him that I still have. I feel it has his energy in it, and it brings me comfort. I hold Kevin's dog, Chloe. The physical act of petting this sweet baby reminds me that not only did I suffer a loss, but she did as well. It helps me to remember that she and I are in this together! I write my thoughts and memories of times shared with my love in a journal. I never want to forget anything and if I feel that I am on the verge of forgetting, I write it down. I take a nap and refresh my soul.

*

MARYELLEN ROACH
MaryEllen's sister Suzette and two nieces, 6-year-old
Vivian and 8-year-old Lillian, died in car accident in 2012

In the beginning, there was nothing that brought me comfort, because it was all too raw and painful. As time has moved on, wearing my sister's clothes helps me feel close to her, which is comforting. I can't handle looking at my sister and nieces' pictures, so instead I like having things around that belonged to them. I also enjoy doing things that make me feel like I'm doing something for them or in their honor. My younger sister has a baby named Elliana or Ellie for short. I felt a lot of happiness when I recently gave Ellie a pair of socks that I had given Lillian when she was a baby. I knew Lillian would be thrilled for Ellie to have her special socks that say "cutie" on the side. It was also comforting because it will help Ellie know her cousins, and in general, things that keep them alive bring me comfort. I also find comfort in posting pictures and stories in a blog or on Facebook. I love sorting through photos and taking time to cherish the memories. I also find comfort in keeping their things exactly as they were.

*

MARY LEE ROBINSON
Mary Lee's 63-year-old husband Pat
died of a sudden cerebral hemorrhage in 2013

My circumstances when my husband died were a little different. We had just moved to a new state and I didn't know many people, other than my other new-to-the-state neighbors (who were almost all neglectful, inconsiderate louts and remain so). Because, in his illness, my husband drastically changed his financial affairs, I thought I had absolutely no money. I had to cancel the final memorial service arrangements I had made. There was no service or gathering. I have no family, beyond three octogenarians in other states. No one was with me in those awful days of the immediate aftermath. No one came. I have a handful of very dear friends who recognized my plight, and sent tangible tokens of sympathy.

Two friends gave me books: One was a collection of daily meditations. The other was a daily devotional. Both gifts were and are cherished and a great deal of help, as are those friends. The only meal I was given was from a neighbor who packaged up her leftovers and gave them to me once. I know she meant well, but yeah, that's what I needed. I needed to sit all alone in my house, eating somebody else's leftovers. She wanted to give me my time alone and privacy. My husband died suddenly. I was drowning in time alone and privacy. What I needed were invitations to join other families. I needed someone to "set an extra plate" for me and give me back some sense of normal life.

I also got hugs. Hugs are good. One can't get too many hugs.

Also, if you observe a condition you think needs attention (the bills are piling up, the weeds are out of control, the Christmas tree isn't up), again, ask! "I see that....fill in the blank...isn't done. Can I help you with it?" And then respect the answer. Nothing was and is more infuriating to me than to have someone come into my home and tell me that the light bulb in my fifteen-foot ceiling is out, or that the dishwasher rack is broken. No DUH!!! I KNOW it's broken. I just can't take care of it myself. I know there are things I need to get rid of. They may be too heavy for me, or I don't know where to take them, or it's emotionally overwhelming. Don't just observe and JUDGE ... help. You may need help too eventually.

Meditation and devotional books brought me comfort, as did meals, hugs, invitations to come visit, soft and peaceful music, a lovely living peace lily. One new friend helped me dispose of my husband's clothes and belongings. The fellas who told me jokes. It's the way men console. They will stand on their heads trying to make a sad person laugh. I didn't always laugh, but I recognized instantly what they were doing, and the caring that was behind it.

Things that brought me comfort include meditational readings, including and especially my Bible, hot baths with lavender and Epsom salts, lighting candles, new age music, wearing my husband's T-shirt and my dad's old robe, wearing mourning jewelry, and buying a very large dog. Also comedy flicks were a vacation from grief. Getting away occasionally for short escapes as well as one or two long ones were restful. Getting out among people and entertaining as I was able. The sound of laughter and voices in my home was immensely helpful. Helping others also helps us to get out of our own heads.

*

ALEXIS VON UTTER
Alexis was 12 when her father Marc
died at age 57 from lung cancer complications

Like some people, and unlike others, my dad was sick for a while in the hospital before he passed, so people would bring meals. But in the first few days after he passed, I just wanted to try to be normal. I didn't want people pitying me, I wanted to feel like I was normal, even though a major change had occurred in my life.

*

HEATHER WALLACE-REY
Heather was 40 when her father John
died suddenly at age 71 of a massive heart attack

For the first few months after Dad died, I held onto quite a few of his possessions; especially things that smelled like him (oh, I know that's weird). I wore his winter coat around in the middle of the summer, and I smelled his shoes (weirder). What brought me the most comfort after my dad died were doing things that were both productive, and in some cases, reminded me of my dad. He was a Buddhist, and often talked about how he'd probably come back as a butterfly. The first summer after he had passed away, I researched and planted and tended a butterfly garden, which I know Dad would have loved.

*

DIANNE WEST
Dianne's 69-year-old husband Vern
died from multiple myeloma in 2010

I wasn't sleeping or eating well, and had no energy or desire to go to the grocery store, so food deliveries were welcomed. Fresh sheets or a soft throw was an unexpected comfort. I slept in Vern's hospital bed or recliner for weeks after he died. Friends were concerned when I shared this, but it was where I felt closest to him. I eventually returned to our bed, but had to pile up clothes and pillows to fill up his side in order to sleep there. Other things that brought comfort included setting up a memorial spot with Vern's urn and mementos, reading my CaringBridge journal entries or sympathy cards, sleeping in one of his shirts, and writing notes to Vern in a journal.

*

CHAPTER ELEVEN

UNDERSTANDING OUR FEARS

We do not fear the unknown. We fear what
we think we know about the unknown.
TEAL SWAN

In the aftermath of loss, many irrational fears consume our thoughts. We become convinced that lightning can strike twice. Your instinct might be to judge us, and tell us lightning won't strike twice, but our brains live in fear of that second strike.

For those of us who have lost a loved one in a car accident, we have a deep fear of cars. When we're a white-knuckled passenger in your car with an outstretched right foot searching for a passenger side brake, you now know why. If someone lost a spouse to pneumonia, a single cough can prompt an immediate doctor visit.

We also fear that we'll forget our loved one, as will the world. We find ourselves listening to their voicemail greeting, videos, scrolling through their phone or computer in an effort to memorize their face, sound of their voice, gestures, and other important elements we fear we might forget. We share our fears with you in this chapter to help you understand why fear plays a dominant role in the aftermath of loss, and how you can help.

The oldest and strongest emotion of mankind is fear,
and the oldest and strongest is fear of the unknown.

H. P. LOVECRAFT

Things We Fear

1. **The future.**
   We fear what the future holds for us in the absence of our loved one. We fear future holidays, future vacations, and future family members never knowing our loved one. We fear making new memories without our loved one.

2. **Losing another loved one.**
   Because losing another loved one can, and does, happen to some, we fear it will happen to us a second time. The thought of facing the same wretched journey all over again strikes terror in our hearts.

3. **Failing to reach you.**
   Because grief heightens our fear of losing another loved one, when we fail to reach you on the phone or the computer, our anxiety begins to build rather quickly.

4. **Traveling in cars/plane/boat.**
   Whether we lose a loved one in an accident or not, traveling in cars or a plane or boat can exacerbate the fear of losing you in a car, plane or boat.

5. **Being alone or growing old alone.**
   We fear never being loved again.

6. **Lifetime repercussions for our loved ones.**
   We fear that others around us feel just as bad as we do. We want to protect them from such pain. Plus, will they recover? How severely will this loss affect them down the road?

7. **Feeling sad forever.**
   The sadness can feel so overwhelming that we fear it will never evaporate. We fear it will never be possible to feel others emotion besides sadness ever again.

8. **Falling apart or feeling "crazy" forever.**
   We fear failing. We fear letting go and allowing ourselves to feel the sorrow, for fear we'll never survive.

9. **Forgetting details about our loved one.**
   We fear we'll forget the smell of their hair, the sound of their voice, their laughter, their little mannerisms, or what their hug feels like.

10. **Our loved one being forgotten by others.**
    We fear our loved one will be forgotten. We also fear future family members who will never know our loved one.

11. **Someone who looks like our love one.**
    When we see someone who resembles our loved one, it steals our breath and is like a kick in the stomach. It's hard to hold the tears back.

12. **The holidays.**
    We fear seeing the empty chair and traditions that will never feel the same.

13. **Dying.**
    If we die, what happens to those we care for? Who will take care of them? Who will wipe their tears?

14. **Returning to work.**
    Will others feel uncomfortable around us? Will they ignore my loss and pretend nothing happened? Will they ask too many questions? Will I be able to function? Will I make it through the day? Will I not make it through the day? What if I can't make it through the day? Will they fire me?

Forget Me Nots

1. **The fear is real.**
   It can cause nightmares, paranoia and obsessive thinking.

2. **Expect irrational fears.**
   This is normal, as sorrow exacerbates or heightens many of our fears. We already know our fear seems irrational, please avoid arguing about it.

3. **We cannot control or "cure" the fears.**
   Simple and loving reassurance really helps; so does engaging us in conversations.

4. **Take time to understand.**
   A fear can be severe. Take time to understand the root of the fear because when you lose patience or judge our fear, it conveys that you think we're crazy. We fear being crazy.

5. **Patience and compassion are key.**
   Having a safe outlet to share and vent our fears will eventually allow us to process and work through them.

My 10 Rules of Grief
By Lynda Cheldelin Fell

1. There are no rules. Period.

2. I will grieve my way. Not your way. My way may not make sense to you, but it doesn't make sense to me either.

3. The grief timeline is long. If I begin to move on in two months, something is wrong. If I begin to move on in two years, be impressed.

4. Hugs are, and always will be, better than words.

5. When you ask me how I am, I will always answer politely. The truth is not pretty.

6. If I question my faith, do not condemn me. It is normal.

7. Yes, I am blessed to have other children. But the pain from losing one is worse than agony.

8. Consider me a patient of Grief United General. The first part of my healing begins with a lengthy stay in the ICU. Treat me accordingly.

9. Do not try to understand my overwhelming emotions. It will exhaust us both.

10. Honor my pain by walking with me, not directing me.

11. I am not a victim, I am grieving. Treat my journey with respect and compassion, for our turn will come.

12. I know this is more than ten rules. That's because grief doesn't ever make sense.

Thoughtful Insight

*

EMILY BAIRD-LEVINE
Emily's 43-year-old brother Don
died from a heart attack in 2004

My biggest fear has been the anticipation of the next loss in life and how I will handle it. I dread the day I have to experience any of this again. Please be patient with us no matter what feelings we share with you. All of our feelings are valid. Be supportive and available, but don't overdo it if you feel discomfort from us.

*

EMILY BARNHARDT
Emily's 20-year-old friend/roommate
Hannah died by suicide in 2014

Fear is something I struggle with in all areas of my life, and one of my deepest fears is losing the people I love. Going through grief can easily heighten that type of fear immensely, because you are currently experiencing just how devastating loss is. Losing Hannah opened an entire new depth of that fear in me, because the pain of losing her is beyond my ability to even put into words. It terrifies me to think of going through this pain again in losing someone else I dearly love, and it terrifies me knowing that this type of nightmare can suddenly begin in a split second when you get that call or hear those words that your loved one is gone.

Since Hannah's death, I've noticed a huge increase in this fear, and it can take me to irrational, paranoid mindsets more often than I like to admit. There are moments, sometimes for no apparent reason at all, when I get hit with this random immense wave of panic that something has happened to one of my friends or family members. It's intensified if I can't reach them. It's oftentimes completely irrational and unjustifiable, as half of the time there's no red flag indicating a need for concern, so I don't know what triggers those random moments when I panic about the safety of someone. All I know is I'll just suddenly get terrified and have a desperate need to know that a certain person is okay.

Thankfully, my loved ones were compassionate and sensitive toward this heightened fear I've experienced, and they've been patient with me in times when I've randomly sent them a frantic, worried text out of the blue. They don't make a big deal about it; they simply respond reassuringly that everything is okay, fully understanding where the anxiety is truly coming from. I've appreciated their patience and understanding with me and the intense fear this loss stirs up in me at times. Given that I lost Hannah to suicide, my fear of people dying can understandably take on a life of its own when someone I know is struggling emotionally.

Volunteer work I've done, my own life experiences, and my field of study has connected me with many people who battle all sorts of addictions, traumas, mental illnesses, etc. I honestly can't count the number of times I've helped talk someone down from suicide or convinced someone to put down the razor they intended to harm themselves with. I'm humbled and thankful that God can use me to help others. I know He put this compassion in my heart for people hurting, so it isn't a burden; I love helping people, and I will always be there for anyone who reaches out or needs support.

Having lost a close loved one to suicide, however, I've noticed that the nervousness and fear I feel in situations where a friend is suicidal or in a dark place has intensified. I have to be careful because I know that the pain of wishing I could've stopped Hannah that night will often lead me to overextend myself and deplete myself in my efforts to save others. I sometimes slip into an irrational mindset of determination to not let anyone else in my life die by suicide. Realistically though, that's not possible; I don't have the power to save everyone around me. When I succumb to that mentality, I get drained very quickly, and it isn't healthy for me. I can't take care of myself if I'm giving everything I have to others. And frankly, I won't be an effective support for someone if I don't take care of myself as well. So, I'm working on maintaining healthy boundaries and knowing my limits. Like the flight attendants say, "We have to put on our own oxygen masks before we help others put on theirs."

My heightened, irrational state of fear after Hannah's death has lessened as time has passed and as I've walked through the grief. I still wrestle with it, of course, so I continue working on it. I know that if I let my fears overtake me and consume me, I'll suffocate from the weight of them, and then I would truly be of no help at all to anyone in my life who needs me.

In supporting someone through grief, be patient with them and sensitive to their fears. If they express a desperate need to make things right after a disagreement between the two of you, it's possible that they are afraid to have that conversation end badly, because they are brutally aware of how short life can be. If they're afraid to do something that could possibly (but rarely) be dangerous, maybe that fear stems from the reality of death they are facing. The examples are endless, so the best thing supporters can do is to try to be empathetic, patient, and sensitive to any anxiety or fear they sense in their loved one.

*

CHRISTINE BASTONE
Christine's sister Elizabeth
died in 2012 at age 38

My worst fear is that my sister will be forgotten. I consider it one of my jobs now, as Liz's big sister, to make sure that she's not.

*

ERICA GALE BELTZ
Erica's 5-year-old son Luke Jordan died in 2002
from a fallen banister in his aunt's driveway

I feared myself. I feared my own reflection and everything it told me. I feared waking up again to face another day that I was so undeserving of. I feared the possibility of my sister not being here tomorrow; I feared the pain my brother was in. I had no idea that this could happen a second time to someone, but I started to find out that it does. I feared my daughter's life and the pain she was in, and not ever being able to stand again.

*

SOPHIA BLOWERS
Sophia was 50 when her mother Amy
died at age 79 of internal bleeding

My biggest fear was falling apart. I think that is why words of affirmation were so very important to me. I needed to hear I was okay, because I did not think I was okay. I thought I was going to fall apart at any time, and if I did, I would not pull myself back together. Arguments, criticism, and harsh demands were the triggers that set me toward a panic attack. I would feel like I did not have control, was not functioning properly or taking care of my family adequately. I could feel my chest tighten and my breathing shorten. Hearing that I was okay, that no matter what I did the people I loved would stay with me, was the key to me beginning to heal. I needed the confidence to go forward in my way, in my time.

*

LYNDA CHELDELIN FELL
Lynda's 15-year-old daughter Aly
died in a car accident in 2009

It's common for those who lose a loved one to become fearful of lightning strike twice. As irrational as it sounds to others, it becomes a daily anxiety we live with. That fear can petrify us, causing us to make decisions in an effort to bubble-wrap and protect our loved ones. Your instinct might be to reassure us that lightning won't strike twice, but it does, and we live in fear of that second strike. To this day, both my husband and I get terribly nervous when any family members, especially the kids, are in the car, whether running errands or going to work. I can hardly focus until I know they're safe. I expected this to ease with time, but we're still waiting. Thankfully, my husband and I have talked about this, and once we realized we both share the same fear, it helps each of us feel less alone though it doesn't diminish the fear.

Since my husband's stroke in 2012, I remain very fearful I'll walk around the corner to find him on the floor. Or I fear he'll never wake up, and I'll find him dead in bed. He just turned fifty, and it's been nearly four years since his stroke, yet my fear is just as strong today as it was in the initial aftermath.

*

MICHELLE DETWILER
Michelle's 19-year-old daughter Emily
died in 2014 due to congenital complications

One of my fears was that I would forget what my daughter looked like, smelled like, or felt like when I hugged her. I can say that after almost two years without her, I have not forgotten any of those things! Another fear was that my other children would die. While this sounds unreasonable, it is a very real fear that causes me anxiety.

*

CHRISTINE DUMINIAK
Christine's 86-year-old mother Ann
died from an aortic aneurysm in 2004

My biggest fear was how I was going to feel when the first holiday came around without my loved one and seeing the empty chair. Others can help by sitting in the empty chair, even if it seems irreverent to do so. It just helps not seeing that chair being filled.

*

SHARON EHLERS
Sharon's best friend Joy died in 2009 at age 52
Sharon's former fiancé John died in 2012 at age 59

One thing John's death did bring to the forefront, although not really a fear, was making sure you have "everything in order," especially if you are a parent. John chose to leave his mother and his children with a financial and legal mess. They were thrust into a world they never should have had to deal with. There was no will. There was no money. Seeing this made me realize that I needed to make sure everything was in place for my own children.

*

ANNAH ELIZABETH
Annah's newborn son Gavin Michael
died 26 minutes following his birth

One of my biggest fears was that I would forget Gavin, and that the world would forget him. Those who were not afraid to say his name and those who were prepared to say his name and then take the time to be with me if that question brought my grief to the surface were some of the greatest blessings I had. One of the other fears is one that we all have, especially those who have experienced the sudden or untimely death of a loved one, is the fear that mishap or misfortune could happen to another of my loved ones. The best way people likely could have helped me, as do the ones who bring me comfort today, would have been to honor the truth that the next second of our earthly life is not guaranteed. I especially find solace in people who believe in hope and that we can not only survive if we are willing, but to go on to thrive. Those who model the truth that we can live our best personal, professional, and philanthropic life following tragedy bring me the greatest inspiration. I am inspired by those who recognize life's fragility and strive not to take it for granted, and by those who remain conscious of life's hope, healing, and happy elements Those are the people who help keep me moving forward.

*

BRENDA KLEINSASSER
Brenda's 88 year-old mother
died from congestive heart failure in 2011

I really thought that I would fall apart when my mother passed. One thing that gives me comfort is that how I am feeling at any given moment is okay. I may not always feel a certain way, but it is okay to feel that way now, as it will not always be that way. That gives me freedom to grieve in my own way.

*

DEANA MARTIN
Deana's only two children, 25-year-old Amanda
and 21-year-old Logan, died in a car accident in 2011

My fears were, and are, growing old alone. My children were supposed to bury me. Who will care for me now when I get old? My granddaughter will be a very young woman by the time I get there, and I don't want her to sacrifice her life to care for me. I fear I will always feel so empty. Will I always long so deeply for my children? Will my heart always feel so heavy?

*

DIANE MCKENZIE-SAPP
Diane's 65-year-old husband Ron
died from renal failure in 2006

I am not afraid to die; I am afraid that the art I have created will not live past me. My rings have made a difference in the world. They were heavenly inspired, and I feel that I am doing what I was born to do. I want them to continue to heal broken hearts long past my time. With my death, I imagine the rings being sold for scrap metal, and tossed into the garbage. I envision those who would never know the relief of these heaven-sent rings.

Early in 2014, I said that the collection of rings I had designed was complete. In November 2014, I was diagnosed with a rare relentless cancer. The doctor had a helpless look when he said, "You have angiosarcoma. It is rare, not much is known about it, and the usual prognosis is three months. I am sorry."

My children and family rallied to research cancer doctors, treatments, herbals, diets and healers. They asked what they could do. To their dismay my only future concern was, "How are the rings going to continue after me?" My children filled orders while I could not, but I had no long-term solution.

I had surgery in December 2014. I face reoccurrence at any time. I was led to a world-renowned doctor at the Texas Medical Center. I am in remission and have a scan every three months, watching for metastasis and suspicious symptoms. I was desperate for a solution to the question, "What will happen with the rings?" I voiced my concern to a higher being. "This was your idea; I was your tool. If it is time for me to go, if the designs are completed, if you have a plan for their continued existence, so be it. It is in your hands." Help is not a coincidence. Mike was selected when I printed all the Maryland patent agents, filling up both sides of forty pages. I spread them out, and stabbed randomly with a pen. I stabbed Mike. I called and asked if he would agent my design patent. He didn't do design patents, and didn't know anyone who did. I suggested if he started doing them he would have the entire field to himself. He began the process with no fees and no guarantees and won my patent. Help is not a coincidence.

Another godsend was Mary Lee Robinson, author of *The Widow or Widower Next Door*. When she came into my life, I found a solution and a kindred spirit. She is a ray of light, outgoing, pragmatic, and the savior for my rings. She promised she would continue the rings after I died. I breathed a breath of fresh air. We would merge our strengths. She is my maven. A maven is a trusted expert in a particular field who seeks to pass knowledge on to others. The word maven comes from Hebrew meaning "one who understands," based on an accumulation of knowledge. Without Mary Lee, the newest rings would not have left the drawing board.

Apparently my creative calling is renewed on a tri-monthly cycle. God's wake-up message says, "Act as if today is the rest of your life; tomorrow is not guaranteed." Thinking that a remarkable collection of remembrance rings was completed, I was divinely corrected, and this bargain was an ingenious approach to gain my attention. Motivated with a ticking-time extension, I designed several new rings.

"Dear Lord, I designed, within the last nine months, five new rings and a pendant. I need to live for two to four more years to get more designs done. The odds are one in a hundred thousand. Are *you* renewing?"

*

MARY POTTER KENYON
Mary's 60-year-old husband David
died of heart failure in 2012

My greatest fear is that I will never be loved again, and yet I am grateful I knew what it was to be truly loved. I am also scared that losing their dad will have lifetime repercussions for my children, particularly my three youngest girls, who were eight, twelve, and fifteen years of age when their dad died. I hate being a single parent and making parenting decisions alone. My youngest is now twelve, and I still worry about her. I have clung to God's promise to never leave me or forsake me, and that brings me great comfort. I really wish there was a village to help me raise my children. My youngest could really use a mentor who is willing to spend time with her. Her dad was her best friend. Honesty really is the best policy. I am surprised sometimes how just being honest brings about some understanding. If I tell someone that going to a wedding is just going to be too difficult for me, it is better than making up an excuse.

*

NANCY REDMOND
Nancy's 40-year-old husband Kevin
died of a heart attack in 2012

My greatest fears have been that everyone who Kevin loved would forget him: Forget how he looked, forget his voice, forget his loving nature, forget his amazing drumming talents, forget his laugh—forget Kevin! I feared not living through these horrible times. I feared going back to work, and I feared facing daunting new financial responsibilities.

*

MARYELLEN ROACH
MaryEllen's sister Suzette and two nieces, 6-year-old
Vivian and 8-year-old Lillian, died in car accident in 2012

For a long time, my biggest fear was running into someone who looked like my sister or the girls when I was in public. I was terrified I would see someone bearing their resemblance, and I would become a huge puddle of tears and emotions, which I would find embarrassing. Those fears led to panic attacks, severe anxiety and fewer shopping trips. Sometimes I felt fear for no particular reason. Now that it's been three years since losing my sister and nieces, I've had time to think about my feelings, and have come to the conclusion that I was feeling the irrational fear because one of my biggest fears already became a reality.

186

*

MARY LEE ROBINSON
Mary Lee's 63-year-old husband Pat
died of a sudden cerebral hemorrhage in 2013

When my husband died, we lived in a new neighborhood with very few houses, and none of them nearby. We had a lot of "up to no good" traffic at night, as kids and dealers found obscurity at the end of our street. While it's a nice neighborhood, it is not densely populated. It looks like your average golf course community, just not many houses yet.

Three things helped: One of the small group of helpful neighbors is a retired police captain who, by habit, drove around the neighborhood at night. He made a point of driving by my house. We had an incident involving a car chase from the main highway into our neighborhood. It was 4 a.m. when the retired police captain called to tell me what was going on. He then told me that not only were the police combing the area for the driver who was now on foot, but he was parked outside in front of my house.

One of my vendors is a retired fire department lieutenant. He didn't live close by, but he would check on me once he realized my situation. He and his wife made it crystal clear that they were available to help. He stepped in to a similar chase episode during the afternoon. He never left my side until the police scanner announced that the driver was caught. Lastly, I can't say enough about the local police department. The officers who patrolled my neighborhood went out of their way to drive by. One officer also made a pointed effort to show up when construction workers were working across the street. He'd pull his car into the drive and leave a hang tag on my door if I was not home. When I was, he'd sit on the front porch with me for a few minutes and talk.

I sent a thank-you to the police department for their extra effort. I got a letter back from the police chief telling me not to hesitate to call if I ever needed them. More heroes. These guys are my heroes.

*

KRISTI SMITH
Kristi's 48-year-old husband Michael
died from cardiac arrest in 2011

One of our biggest fears is that people will forget about our heartache, and a couple of weeks after the loss, we will be left all alone. We need people to remember our loved one and validate our pain.

*

HEATHER WALLACE-REY
Heather was 40 when her father John
died suddenly at age 71 of a massive heart attack

My biggest fear after Dad passed away was that I had become certifiably crazy. The things that I did and said, the ways I reacted to things, and the absolutely asinine things that went through my head only furthered my belief that I was completely off my rocker.

*

DIANNE WEST
Dianne's 69-year-old husband Vern
died from multiple myeloma in 2010

I felt it was so very important for me to do this right ... to set an example of how to grieve, to honor our love, to honor my husband. I know now that was a pretty ridiculous goal; there is no right way to grieve. I feared failing. I feared falling into depression. I feared dying. I feared living. I felt so very alone and yet I had caused it because of the façade I had created.

*

CHAPTER TWELVE

WHAT WE WANT YOU TO KNOW

Love and compassion are necessities, not luxuries.
Without them, humanity cannot survive.
DALAI LAMA

Every journey through loss is unique, just like our fingerprints. As if loss itself isn't hard enough to understand, two people can face the exact same loss and handle it completely differently based upon past experiences, different beliefs, desires and tolerances.

Why is it important for you to understand our journey? In the wake of every loss is a new transition for the living. And like the ripple effect along water's surface, our inevitable transition impacts those around us.

So what exactly is the hardest part of our journey, and how can you help us work through it? In this chapter, each writer shares what they find the hardest parts and why. Your ability to support us as we weather the transition depends upon how much you understand, and whether you are willing to help our transition, or hinder it.

The ultimate lesson all of us have to learn is unconditional love,
which includes not only others but ourselves as well.
ELISABETH KÜBLER-ROSS

Forget Me Nots

1. **Just like a fingerprint.**
   Every journey is unique; no two are alike.

2. **We miss you.**
   Loneliness is common because people tend to avoid us.

3. **You aren't carrying our saddle.**
   Avoid judging our progress or whether we're grieving "properly."

4. **We exhaust easily.**
   Avoid trying to distract us by keeping us busy. Allow us to set our own schedule.

5. **It will always hurt.**
   The finality of our loss will always be hard for us.

6. **Our new normal.**
   Our daily routine will be significantly altered, and it takes time to figure out what our new routine will be.

7. **It takes time.**
   When we lose our loved one, we lose our world. Transition is inevitable, but will happen slowly.

8. **Think before you speak.**
   Just love us, and accept us where we are in the process.

9. **Time doesn't heal all wounds.**
   The only cure for grief is to grieve.

10. **We truly thank you.**
    We're very grateful for all of your support, even if we don't show it.

Even a small star can shine in darkness.
FINISH PROVERB

Thoughtful Insight

*

EMILY BAIRD-LEVINE
Emily's 43-year-old brother Don
died from a heart attack in 2004

The hardest part is feeling isolated, even while around other people, when they are uncomfortable with me having lost my brother or not knowing what to say or do.

*

EMILY BARNHARDT
Emily's 20-year-old friend/roommate
Hannah died by suicide in 2014

Aside from the actual loss, of course, the hardest thing I faced in my grief was loneliness. Living in an area where I had no family, my only possible sources of physical support were my friends and my community, who had their own lives and responsibilities, as well, and couldn't always be the support I needed. Generally speaking though, loneliness in grief doesn't only come from a lack of support. There are many other factors that can cause a deep, crippling feeling of loneliness. One of those other factors, for me, was the adjustment of living alone. I'd never lived alone until after Hannah passed. We lived together for a few years up until she passed, and even on the nights she stayed with her boyfriend, I still didn't experience living alone. Even on the nights when I went to bed and she wasn't there, there was still evidence of her life there. Sometimes, I'd go to bed alone, but wake up in the morning to her making noise in the kitchen or seeing her in her bed asleep as I made breakfast. I lovingly picked on her for leaving me alone many nights to stay with her boyfriend, but I know now that I honestly had no idea what alone really felt like at that time. I didn't know what alone felt like until I was truly alone in an apartment for two. Before she passed, if I came home to an empty apartment, I knew she was either out, in class or at work, and even if she was gone, I always found comfort in the evidence I saw of her presence there: her books lying around, her clothes thrown across the furniture, or her dishes in the sink.

I remember talking to a friend the day before Hannah took her life, and joked about how she always nailed my pet-peeves whenever she left lights on in our apartment or left dirty dishes sitting on the counter, table, or the ottoman by our couch. The tiny ants that ensued would drive me nuts! Now that she's gone, words can't really express my sorrow and hate over ever feeling annoyed by that, because I would honestly give anything in the world to come home and see those things again. I'd give anything to pick up after her and kill hundreds of ants because she left food out. I'd give anything to come home and see her face and, even if she wasn't there, to at least see evidence that she recently was.

I remember those moments I faced every single day walking into our apartment after she had passed. I remember opening our door to complete darkness, because she hadn't been there to accidentally leave the light on. I remember the way that I would stop in my tracks and feel my heart sink when I saw that everything in our apartment was exactly as I had left it—no new misplaced items, no pillows rearranged, no chair pulled slightly out from the table, no cup on the counter or blanket thrown across the couch cushions.

The door of our apartment would shut behind me, and I can still remember that deafening silence and the haunting stillness that filled the air of our apartment after she was gone. I eventually had to shut her bedroom door, because looking at her room and belongings was too painful. But then, her closed door became the most noticeable thing in the entire apartment. I knew I couldn't stay there, but it took me a few months to handle being able to move. I couldn't handle the idea of having another roommate. It was as if the "best friend and roommate" title was sealed off from newcomers until further notice. So I moved into a one-bedroom apartment. Even though I was in a new apartment, the adjustment of living alone was extremely tough. I wasn't used to never hearing my own voice in my apartment. I was used to conversation, laughter, music, cuddling and interaction. Going to bed alone and waking up alone, each and every day, was a brutally painful adjustment. I'll honestly never forget that eerie and unfamiliar silence that lingered noticeably in the air of our apartment on those dark days and nights after her death.

There's also often a feeling of loneliness in the bereaved due to the fact that the experience of grief is unique and individual. It's frankly impossible for anyone to understand an individual person's experience of grief, unless they are in that person's exact shoes, at that exact moment. The uniqueness of our grief can feel unbearably lonely and extremely isolating, at times.

I remember feeling out of place, as if I didn't really fit in — in my relationships, in the world or in the "me," and life that I'd previously known. I felt lost and misplaced in a world I desperately still wanted to be a part of, but couldn't seem to make sense of anymore. Even in my closest relationships, there was still distance. I wanted to bridge that distance, but I could never find the words to accurately depict what I was experiencing. It was like I was in a parallel universe.

I remember that sinking weight in feeling that it was pointless to try to explain or even talk about what I was going through. Part of me gave up trying to talk about it at one point, simply because I knew that those to whom I was talking couldn't relate. I was afraid that talking about Hannah would distance me from my community more so than I'd already observed. Carl Jung describes this all too accurately in his statement, "Loneliness does not come from having no people about one, but from being unable to communicate the things that seem important to oneself."

I only got through that painful season because I knew I wasn't ever truly alone. I knew God was near to me, even in the moments where I felt furthest from Him. I clung to the knowledge and belief that He was with me. No matter how alone I felt, I found strength in knowing I wasn't. I focused on Him and I focused on the solid, supportive relationships I did have in my life.

*

CHRISTINE BASTONE
Christine's sister Elizabeth
died in 2012 at age 38

The hardest part of my loss is the seemingly little things that I can no longer do. I can no longer pick up the phone, and call my sister. We can't email back and forth. I can't see her, hug her or take her picture. There will be no new pictures of her, ever.

Grief doesn't end in a week or two, a month or two, or even a year or two. People are so impatient for grief to be over. While grief changes, it's never going to be over. Please be patient, and accept grievers where they are.

Grief does not proceed in a straight line, and that's what makes it so confusing. It's very messy and all over the place, so please don't expect it to be all nice and neat.

In my opinion, there are no stages of grief. And the denial, anger, bargaining, depression, and acceptance stages that are frequently talked about with regards to grief were originally meant for terminally ill patients, not people who are grieving. Please don't try and fit grief into orderly, predictable, consecutive stages. It's not your place to decide how a griever should grieve; it's theirs. Encourage them to do what is comforting to them, and to avoid what is painful for them—even if it's what wouldn't comfort you, or what would be painful for you—even if you think it's silly.

Grief is normal and natural. It is not a weakness. It is not a mental illness. It is simply the price of love. So please don't act like it's abnormal or unnatural. Contrary to popular belief, grief doesn't end at the funeral; it begins there. Those first few days? You are in such shock. And most people rally around you. There is all this support. That helps so much. And then you go home after the funeral is over, and it feels like everyone has disappeared. That's when grieving really begins. Society is obsessed with us getting over it and moving on. Well, that's never going to happen for me! In order for me to move on, I have to leave my sister behind, and I am unwilling to do that. I will learn how to cope with it better, and it will get less awful. But until I die and see her again, I'm not going to get over it.

At one point or another, everyone will lose a loved one to death. While there is no way to fully prepare for it, it's very difficult to learn so much about grief while grieving. As a society, we need to educate our children, teenagers, and young adults on this very important subject. As individuals, it would be good to at least read up a little on the subject, and have a few ideas about where you can locate resources that you will need when the time comes.

Grief will not be denied. It can be ignored, delayed, or pushed aside for a while. The only cure for grief is to grieve. Eventually it demands that you deal with it. When the time comes, give yourself time to be ready, but don't wait too long. You can't deny something that refuses to be denied.

Love lives on. It doesn't die when a person does. Most of the time love needs to be expressed. So when grievers talk about their loved ones, write about their loved ones, or post about their loved ones, please do not complain about that. They are only expressing their love, remembering their loved one, and making sure that they aren't forgotten.

People aren't replaceable. We carry a piece of every one we have ever cared about in our heart. And even when they die, or leave, there isn't anyone else who can fill that space. Our hearts are big, and we can care about many people at the same time. But nobody is replaceable. That is just a myth many people believe.

*

ERICA GALE BELTZ
Erica's 5-year-old son Luke Jordan died in 2002
from a fallen banister in his aunt's driveway

The hardest part of the journey, for a long time, was the initial aftermath and the toll it took on us all. It was literally as if an atomic bomb had been dropped, and we somehow had been left in the ashes and rubble. Although we didn't see the rescue choppers in the distance, they were nearing. The pastor brought the young mom, who had just lost her little boy to murder, to the funeral home. She gave me a book, *Safe in the Arms of God*, and it became my bible. My mom had given me a book called *Simple Abundance*; it really spoke to me. I would read ahead several days at a time. Someone else gave me a journal and shared a powerful story, so I began journaling. I decided I would write to Luke. I'm so thankful I have those entries to reflect on. While I was not faithful in daily or consistently writing, it holds some precious moments that would have forever been lost.

We watched the DVD from the funeral home over and over. I knew how much work was needed in gathering Luke's pictures, and that made it extra special. It was something we all were able to do. Family and friends made another CD with our favorite "Luke music," and we listened to it over and over.

After I attended my first bereaved parent support group, I had an idea about what to add to my survivor tool box. The other parents who attended gave me the names of books they read, and told me about the ways they each survived. I listened intently. These people were still alive and eager to help me. I needed to find out how this was possible. I also received the book, *Stacey*, written by Stacey's father, the pastor who led Luke's funeral. The next month I went back to the group, and was given a book, *Children of the Dome*. Rosemary Smith, the author, lost two sons in the same car accident. She not only survived, but started sending cards to other bereaved parents. She attended funerals, and before long, she had reached out to more than 10,000 families. I was in total amazement of her strength and courage. She was honoring her sons' lives; they would never be forgotten. I was searching for something so Luke would always be remembered. I thought I needed something huge, like a baseball stadium, but this was beautiful. I had no money and no will to live, but I began to write. Although I had no idea at that time, hope was starting to creep in. TCOTD (book) told the stories of more than twenty families. At night, my sister and I would take turns reading them aloud to each other. We wailed and cried for each of them, as we grew to love their children. Sometimes a few days would go by without opening it because the pain and stories were just too much, but, we always came back to it.

A mother and father, who lost their son in a military night-training exercise, led a small group. Because information about the accident was classified, the parents never got to see their son again. But I laughed when they said in the description of his belongings were his Goofy character boxers. Their ability to start to heal and find some joy in the boxers their son was wearing brought his funny wit above the wreckage. It spoke to me.

I was told about a conference organized in Kentucky, and I was invited to go. I was so excited, and could not wait to meet other parents, especially author Rosemary Smith. As time drew closer, I began to back out. I was drinking a lot more, and slept most of the day we were supposed to leave. I called to cancel. They came and picked me up anyway. I was a mess, but they shared with me, loved on me, and never even hinted they knew what bad shape I was in. I attended my first candle lighting, and really sobbed. I sat and watched Rosemary give an opening speech, and could not believe I was there. I heard Cindy Bullen sing songs from her CD, *Somewhere Between Heaven and Earth*. Cindy's daughter was a spitfire redhead, who died just after turning eleven years old, due to complications from Hodgkin lymphoma. I could not wait to share it with the world. It is still in my toolbox.

*

SOPHIA BLOWERS
Sophia was 50 when her mother Amy
died at age 79 of internal bleeding

The finality of the loss was, and still is, hard for me to get my hands around — the fact that I cannot pick up the phone and call when something wonderful happens; the fact that I don't have that person to cry to, who will forgive my tears or angry outbursts. I struggle with these things constantly. I have found some comfort by talking to Mom as if I am in the room with her. I ask her questions. I tell her my stories. I whine to her when life is not going the way I want. I also found someone who loved her as much as I do, and talk to them often about her. I keep her present in my world and in my heart.

*

LYNDA CHELDELIN FELL
Lynda's 15-year-old daughter Aly
died in a car accident in 2009

The hardest part of my loss was every single breath. Yes, just breathing was painful. I was suddenly an alien in a foreign world void of all color, sound and beauty. I was deaf and blind to the world around me for the first three years. And then my dear sweet hubby suffered a terrible stroke, thrusting me into a different kind of grief.

It's terrifically hard when one is faced with loss to suddenly lose their support circle, too. But it happens. People avoided me out of discomfort. They felt like they *had* to say something if we crossed paths and, of course, there are no words. People would actually cross to the other side of the street if they saw me coming just to avoid me. There are no words one can say that is capable of soothing such sorrow. They didn't know that all I needed was a hug and a shoulder to cry on.

*

MICHELLE DETWILER
Michelle's 19-year-old daughter Emily
died in 2014 due to congenital complications

The most difficult thing about my loss was that I lost more than my child; I lost my community and my life when my daughter died. I had spent nineteen years taking care of a severely disabled and medically fragile child. She had needs that required nursing care for many years. She also had a large list of doctors, therapists, and school personnel who supported her through her life. We saw these people from once a month, to once a week, to every day. What would I fill my life with now that she was gone?

*

CHRISTINE DUMINIAK
Christine's 86-year-old mother Ann
died from an aortic aneurysm in 2004

The hardest part for me was not to be able to talk to and do certain activities with my loved one. So even though at first I did not want to do these same activities with other people, I thought I would give it a try anyway. This way I would still be participating in an activity I really enjoyed, so the loss would not be a double one. At first I had to put on my happy face when participating in these activities with others. I greatly missed my loved one, even though I was going through the motions. However, over time, I found that I was becoming closer to the people who I was doing these activities with. I found that if I asked them questions about themselves and their personal lives, that we felt closer to one another, and little by little, the loneliness that I was feeling in the beginning was not as strong. Even though no one will ever take the place of your loved one, doing things with other people, and forming new and closer friendships, can definitely put a bandage over the hole in your heart over time.

*

SHARON EHLERS
Sharon's best friend Joy died in 2009 at age 52
Sharon's former fiancé John died in 2012 at age 59

When I first learned about Joy's suicide, nighttime was the worst for me. For some reason I was afraid to close my eyes, because I didn't want to imagine how she had killed herself. For a while, I kept playing it over and over in my head. I just kept walking myself through what I created in my own mind as "the events." I just kept seeing it over and over again. It was hard to sleep those first few weeks and months. With John, every moment of every day was the hardest. My brain couldn't stop thinking about him. I went to work, and tried to get through the day, but it was always with me. I think because I had loved him from the depths of my soul that the grief just became a part of my DNA. I found when I was alone I was able to release the pain through my tears. I yearned for the alone time because being around people all day just made it much harder.

*

ANNAH ELIZABETH
Annah's newborn son Gavin Michael
died 26 minutes following his birth

What was the hardest part of my loss? Probably all of it. For different reasons, at different times. That said, there were a few things that I learned along the way that were especially helpful. We've all said it at one time or another, "I know how you feel, I've been there before." Right? I once said that to my sister when she was lamenting during a difficult time in her life. "You've never been where I am," my sis shouted at me. "My life's a living hell." Right then and there I had an "aha" moment. "You're right, Sis," I said, "I've never been in the exact same place you are, but I've been right next door; everyone's hell is different, but everyone has their own living hell."

*

DAPHNE GREER
Daphne's 5-year-old daughter Lydia
died in a car accident in 2008

Blindsided with tragedy, I was thrust into a foreign world in my early thirties. Coming from a fairly carefree and grief-free life, losing my daughter gave me instant turmoil and unbelievable sorrow. My perfect world, as I knew it, had been shattered. My family, my hopes and dreams, were all stripped away from me within seconds. I was lost, and became a stranger to myself, transforming from the familiar life I once knew. My grief was incredibly lonely and very isolating. No one could understand what I was going through after my daughter died, causing me to retreat to the safety of my bedroom closet. I was desperate to find that connection with others who knew what I was feeling.

Reintegrating back into life was a strenuous challenge. I felt like I didn't fit in anywhere with old friends and new. I felt the pressure to put on an act, to try to be the funny, free-spirited person I always had been, just to accommodate the feelings of others, and it was miserable.

As time moved on, I was forced to go to places and events that I didn't want to attend, and heard the terrifying and hurtful words from others that I needed to "move on." I was suffering feelings I had never experienced before. Frightened from my new reality, I experienced pain throughout my body from places I didn't know existed. Not just physical pain, but a deep emotional and spiritual bruising, likely to never return to its original state. From keeping your sanity, to managing a marriage hanging by threads, and trying to parent other children, all the while dealing with a rollercoaster of emotions and scary unknowns, is the most challenging endeavor I've ever done. Sadly, it requires daily effort to manage grief and maintain all other aspects of our life. Grief takes courage, faith, strength, hope and most importantly perseverance.

*

BRENDA KLEINSASSER
Brenda's 88 year-old mother
died from congestive heart failure in 2011

I felt like I was on this journey all by myself. The world continued, but I was looking from the outside. The bereaved want to know how they will be able to go on without their loved one. Grieving is a process, and it is different for each person. When you are going through something like this, at first anyway, it is like you are not part of the equation, but that you are looking from the outside while the world continues. Every day you strive to honor that person who is gone by living your life. Some days are easier to accomplish that task than others. There may be days when you are so consumed with grief, that all you can do is cry. There may be no rhyme or reason for it, but it is part of the process. It is perfectly normal to feel this way. Having a good cry can be very cleansing to the soul. Losing someone, especially a best friend, makes you re-evaluate so many things in your life. How will I make it through another anniversary of their death, without sobbing the whole day long? How will I truly honor their memory? One of the things that I strive to be is half the woman that my mother was. She told me that someday I would be. I realize I am nowhere near that destination, but I still try every day to reach for that. I also struggle with the isolation of having to be by myself every holiday. You would think that every year would get easier, but really you are learning to adjust. This journey is like no other, and each person deals with it differently. It's nice to know that there are others out there who belong to this special club—one that no one really ever wants to belong to.

Losing a loved one is one of the hardest things that a person can go through. I truly thought that I would be destroyed by the passing of my mother. I knew her death was eminent, but that did not make it any easier to face. When I finally decided that I could no longer handle this on my own, I asked hospice to step in and help. The counselor was absolutely wonderful. The thing she kept telling me was that my mother was so concerned about how I would be able to handle things once she was gone. My mother and I were extremely close and so much alike in many ways. I aspire to be like her. She was a woman of great character, and to see her change because of not wanting to eat anymore was just heartbreaking. Her brain cells were starting to die, so her thought process was not clear, and she was insisting that she was seeing things that were not there. I would say, "If what you were seeing is making you afraid, we could try and help with that." Her personality changed so drastically, especially toward the last few days of her life. She became combative, which was so uncharacteristic for her. It was hard to hear those words from the nursing staff at the home. I found myself hoping that she would be able to go to Heaven soon, as she was suffering. She would ask me how much longer, and I would tell her that it would be soon. That was probably three or four days before she passed. After she passed, I brought her dress for the funeral to the home. I saw her finally at peace. My best friend was gone from this earth.

*

DEANA MARTIN
Deana's only two children, 25-year-old Amanda
and 21-year-old Logan, died in a car accident in 2011

The hardest part of my loss is missing my children, and missing who I was with them in my life. I miss their voices, their energy, their touch and their hugs. I miss the little things, and I hate the big things like holidays without them here! It is also very hard to raise my daughter's little girl, who is now eight years old. My heart aches for her loss, and I pray I am being the best grandma/mommy I can. I want her to have a wonderful life, and I want to be able to keep her mommy's and her uncle's memories alive for her; she was only three when they died.

This journey has been one of horror and great trauma, stripping away my identity of Amanda and Logan's mother. It took a long while to understand that I am still my children's mother, and nothing will ever change that. I have felt every feeling, pondered everything that could possibly be pondered about including the whys, if onlys, and I should have, could have and would have. I have beat myself up for stuff that was no way in my control.

Our brains are hardwired to attempt to make sense out of things; when we look at a picture we look for patterns. I have spent endless hours trying to make sense out of the senseless. My belief system was shaken to the core; I don't know what I believe anymore. I used to believe that everything in life, even the tough stuff, was working together for my good. I feel a small flicker of this returning after almost five years, but it is quickly squelched by the overpowering voice that says, "How can this be true? How could my children being crushed to death in a horrific auto accident by a semi-truck be for my good or anyone's good?"

I don't know if there is a God, or an all-powerful creator, or possibly we are an alien experiment. I used to believe we were born with a plan of how our lives would play out, and certain people crossing our path to teach us. How and why would I choose this pain? What is it teaching me?

I have learned that there is a group of very loving and kind individuals on this journey with me, who recognized me in the crowd and invited me into their circle. In the circle is unconditional love, understanding and support. No one who enters this circle will be alone again, except in their own mind. There is healing in this circle, there are great teachers and sages in this circle, but alas there are no answers. There are no elders who have figured out the secrets that will make the pain go away. The elders who are in the circle still hurt and cry — they still long for their loved ones. The elders tell us it will get easier, that the pain will become more manageable and less frequent.

Some are afraid to enter the circle, for to feel love or joy again means they are forgetting their loved one. Their pain is all that binds them to their precious one. There is not an elder alive who could convince these on the outside looking in any different; only time and continued experiences will slowly teach them that holding onto the pain is not holding on to their love.

Love never dies, and the elders and the sages who have gone before teach us that the bond can never be severed. They teach us that rebuilding our lives in honor of our loved ones, being in a place of service to others, doing deeds with pure love and joy and pride for your loved one, is what heals. Slowly albeit, but healing does take place little by little. Holding onto the pain is what blocks the love from flowing in your life and between you and your loved one. What is love but energy, and energy must flow; it is when it is blocked that the light cannot return. Open the channels in whatever way that works for you, but open your heart and embrace the love from within the circle and from your loved one who led you to the circle for comfort and teachings.

*

DIANE MCKENZIE-SAPP
Diane's 65-year-old husband Ron
died from renal failure in 2006

The song "All By Myself," by Celine Dion sums it up for me — I don't want to be all by myself anymore. Once, it was okay but after I found my partner it was not. "Don't want to be all by myself. Don't want to be all by myself. Don't want to be all by myself ...." (clicking my heels together), and still I am all by myself. The hardest part of loss for me is being alone, without someone having your back. For older women, it feels like going out without your purse, and for the younger women it feels like not having your cellphone — forever.

We lived near the ocean, and visited often. If you have walked barefoot at the edge of the vast ocean, you know the hypnotic lure of standing at water's edge as waves massage your legs and toes, and the sand under your feet washes away. After a storm, we would walk together making fleeting footprints in the sand, and searched for shiny glass and pastel shells. Someone I loved held my hand. We stopped and faced the ocean, letting go of everything but waves, sun, the sand, and a few screeching seagulls. We laughed together when one of us lost our balance, and the other pulls them to safety. Sunlight and security and the feeling of "it's you and me against the world" prevailed.

Walking alone, making solo footprints in the sand, I stop and face the ocean, letting go of everything but waves, sun, the sand and a few screeching seagulls. But now I stand there transfixed, watching the endless waves and suddenly realize I'm ankle-deep in clutching sand, and the waves keep pulling the world from under me.

And there is no one to pull me back into safe arms, no one to keep me from falling. No one.

*

MARY POTTER KENYON
Mary's 60-year-old husband David
died of heart failure in 2012

I need to take better care of myself. This is my constant lament since my husband's death. He would have wanted me to. I'm not very good at it, considering I've spent most of my adult life caring for others. But I'm learning to give myself some quiet time, and try not to be too hard on myself.

Cumulative losses piling up one after another had to have affected my grieving process. I first lost my mother. Seventeen months later, I lost my husband. Seventeen months after that, I lost my grandson. Some days, I thought I might be going mad, so I use my pain to help others. I do public speaking on finding hope in the darkness of grief, and I've written about my own journey in an effort to help others. This helps me, too.

Everyone will experience loss at some point in their lives. It is a universal truth. By sharing your grief journeys, it might help someone face their own someday.

The path of grief can be a lonely one, because no one else quite understands our loss, especially those who have never lost anyone. I think we all make conscious choices when grieving. We can wallow in it, or we can make something of it. I chose to make something of it by speaking and writing about finding hope in the darkness of loss. Trust your gut and your heart. I believe our bodies and minds know how to heal, and we are built to withstand loss. I have become much stronger in my faith through multiple losses. I am not the same person I once was, but I love who I have become.

*

NANCY REDMOND
Nancy's 40-year-old husband Kevin
died of a heart attack in 2012

When offering your support to a grieving person, there is no support that you can offer them that will be viewed as doing "the wrong thing." Every single thing you can offer *from a loving heart* is appreciated and noticed. I may not remember at the moment to thank you, but I promise you, you have touched my heart and my soul. This journey has taught me many things, but the greatest gift I can pay forward is to take what I have learned and put it into practice when it becomes my turn to support someone I love on their grief journey. I have learned that many days, I don't recognize my life (or even me!) when I look into the mirror. I haven't been easy to comfort many times, and I expected others to intuitively know what I needed, when I didn't know myself, which made me angry and crabby. I regret those moments, and I sincerely hope I have expressed that remorse to those who tried their hardest. The best thing you can do is to *LOVE* the griever through the darkest days of their lives, knowing that one day, they will be called upon to support and love you on your own journey.

I have learned that asking for help, in no way, makes me weak or incompetent—it makes me human. I have learned to let go and let others love me though this. They may not do it the way I would normally do things (after all, normal *is* overrated!), but they are offering from the heart. Nothing is big or small when you're offering assistance and love to a griever.

I have seen lifetime friendships end on this journey, and I have seen those relationships replaced with even stronger bonds of love in the new friendships that have come into my life. I have fallen many times, and each time, I have found the strength to pick myself up and move on. At other times, I have looked back at my journey with pride and love for myself when I have seen myself find strength I didn't even know I possessed. I have felt great pride when my children told me they were incredibly proud of the way I handled things, and how strong I had been for them. I have three incredibly loving, brave children, so for them to honor me by saying these words to me, means the world to me.

Since the loss of my husband, I have been called upon to comfort others in various stages and avenues of grief. I truly hope I have been a better support to them based on my own experience. I know that the greatest gift you can offer a griever is your presence, and I truly hope I have been there enough for those loved ones I have attempted to comfort in their grief journeys. I have learned that it is not what you say to a griever, but most often, what is not said but felt is what counts the most.

I fear I've failed miserably but I truly hope I have emphasized my gratitude to those who carried me when I could no longer walk this road. I'm certain I haven't expressed my thanks nearly enough for all they did for me, but my heart and soul will never forget.

The hardest part of my loss is missing Kevin's presence in my everyday existence. I miss his text messages, I miss his phone calls, I miss hearing his ringtone on my phone. I miss kissing him, I miss his arms holding me and keeping me safe. I miss our excursions when I'd say, "I'm bored—take me somewhere!" I miss sleeping with him and snuggling in a warm bed. People have tried to fill that void for me, and I love them for it. But only Kevin could be "my Kev," and make me feel the way he did.

None of us are provided a reference manual for this horrible thing called grief but if God thinks I can handle this journey, I do, too. If you're called upon to help a griever, obviously God knows you have a special gift to offer . . . give that person the gift of *you*.

*

MARY LEE ROBINSON
Mary Lee's 63-year-old husband Pat
died of a sudden cerebral hemorrhage in 2013

Our current culture hasn't the vaguest notion about what to do with or for a griever. We used to know. It was commonly understood that we should surround a griever with love and prayers and casseroles. The void the griever is feeling, commencing with the death of a loved one, is emotional, spiritual and practical, and palpable.

Communities rallied to help sand off the rough edges of that void. Knowing that energy is low when grieving, people would pay calls to the house, even after the ceremonies were long over. Grievers were given time to adjust to their new circumstances. Now, in our hurry-up, disenfranchised society, we get, "It's been forty-eight hours; you're okay now, right?" Grief lasts forever; deep grief lasts much longer than people now realize. It's not uncommon or abnormal for deep grief to last twelve to twenty-four months. Complicated grief, with extenuating circumstances, can last even longer.

Death has been distanced from us, with our sanitary hospital rooms and our soothing hospice facilities. Death seldom happens at home, and is never remembered at home now. Once upon a time, the funerals were in the parlor, with the body lying in rest right there inside the home.

Even our pets are put down by professionals now and cremated, just like us. The EPA frowns on burying the family dog in the backyard. So we don't think about death much anymore, and wasn't that the whole point?

We have this weird notion that death only happens to other people, that it only happens in other families. One friend's adult daughter actually said that to her newly widowed mother, a nurse. She was throttled at her daughter's naiveté. How does that work?

We seem to think that if we ignore it, and if we ignore grievers, it will never happen to us. Good luck with that! It behooves all of us to learn again how to help the newly (and not-so-newly) bereaved. To learn that customs and rituals and sometimes idiosyncrasies are healing, not morbid. We've tossed aside some mourning customs, wearing black, draping doorways, wearing mourning jewelry, allowing a yearlong period of reduced activities and more. We've tossed them aside, and yet? And yet the human spirit will demand what it needs. A loss needs to be mourned, fully and deeply. Look around you at all the improvised roadside memorials that have popped up, the memorial tattoos, the rear view window memorial decals, the cremation pendants (yup, that's what that little vial around someone's neck is) that are now in fashion. We aren't supposed to mourn anymore, and yet we can't help ourselves. It's normal. It's natural. It's fitting.

The bone piercing isolation and loneliness was, and occasionally still is, utterly devastating. I miss my husband's company and his demonstrative affection. I also deeply miss my best two sounding boards and cheerleaders, my dad and my husband. They both convinced me that I could fly, if I just made up my mind to do that. It is hard not having their unshakable belief in me in the dimension of the living. I miss their advice and the sense of emotional and actual physical security. Both my Chief of Security officers walked off the job! The void they left is immense.

I've found help in new friendships, and I've taken some measures to keep myself and my home safe and secure. These are reassuring, indeed, but they don't talk to me. Dad and Pat could always talk me down from worry, talk me off the ledge so to speak.

I expected grief to be hard. I did not expect the piling on and the judgment from other people who came. It made the worst situation of my life so much worse than it already was. It absolutely blindsided me. I didn't see it coming, because some of the things that were said and some of the things that were done were things I never, ever did; it would never have occurred to me to be so cruel. One person in my group of new neighbors actually spread rumors that I should not have used my husband's advanced directive. In essence, I was accused of murder, according to three lawyers. This person claimed that my husband, through eye movements, communicated the "he wanted to live." It never happened. There was a "no visitors" order in place because of his condition in ICU, and he was in a coma. His eyes weren't open. Those rumors came back to me, and stuck a knife in my heart. It was another example of someone applying their own standards to a situation that was not their own, and about which they lacked a lot of information.

All I can do, all any of us can do, is keep putting one foot in front of the other. My grandfather's favorite saying just popped into my head: "Can't never did anything!"

My fondest wish is that we become a culture who again knows how to comfort and support those among us who have lost a part of their hearts. To not do so is heartless. Too often, in my own grief journey, I have felt as though I was being kicked when I was already down, further down than I'd ever been before. It is wise to learn the art of grieving well, and consoling well. It will aid us in our coming losses, and we will all have them.

*

MARYELLEN ROACH
MaryEllen's sister Suzette and two nieces, 6-year-old
Vivian and 8-year-old Lillian, died in car accident in 2012

I never knew what grief was fully like, even though I had lost all my grandparents, some friends and acquaintances. When my sister and nieces died in 2012, I was forcefully thrown into the grief world. We were all very close, and my world was shattered. I began writing to work through my feelings, and then realized it may help a non-griever to understand more of what it is like. Here is some of what I wrote, I hope it helps.

When someone dies who is a big part of your life and heart, the pain is truly indescribable. Loss of a close loved one is life-changing. Nothing looks the same after a close loss — not even your own face in the mirror. You don't feel like the same person, because you aren't. No matter how badly you want everything to go back to normal, it never will be the same. Grief takes over your life and every thought you have; it's overwhelming and can be completely consuming. There are emotions associated with grief that I never knew existed, and have no way to describe. It's a nightmare you can't wake up from. Every single moment, whether awake or asleep, is consumed with the thought that you won't see that person for the rest of your life. You not only grieve because that person isn't here now, you grieve the future without them also. Every hope and dream for that person is gone. Every holiday, birthday, and special occasion brings with it the blatant fact they aren't here, and it brings extremely bittersweet memories of when they were.

Some days you can wake up and feel okay, but then hear, see, smell, or remember something that will put your entire day back into the darkness of grief. Although we can control ourselves, grief can be like a lead blanket we just can't get out from under. Grief can steal every ounce of purpose and hope you have ever felt, and it makes everything more difficult. Simple daily tasks become huge chores.

Time becomes different as well. A few months after the accident, I was talking with a griever who had lost their father two years before and I thought, "Oh, it's been two years, so you're doing okay." I thought that because I still didn't fully understand the impact, and was a griever trying to hang onto the same non-griever mentality I had prior. Of course they weren't doing okay; it had only been two years. Two years is a very small amount of time when someone has been part of your entire life, like that griever's dad. People say time heals all wounds; they are wrong. Time only allows a scab to form, and stops the immediate gush of blood. After three and a half years, I must say the scabs on my heart are still thin. Pictures, certain memories, smells, songs, movies, and many other things will scrape, and blood will flow, and it takes several days and sometimes weeks, to scab over again. My heart will never be healed while I'm on Earth, but I pray that in time the scab will become thicker. Full healing will only come when I am reunited with Suzette, Lillian and Vivian in Heaven; I truly look forward to that glorious day that will come in God's time.

As you can see, grief is extremely complex, and although no two grievers are exactly the same, many have the same type of experiences I just described. Being a support for a griever is a difficult job because again no two grievers are exactly the same, so there is no blanket statement or action that will work for everyone. I would suggest that as a support, you be as loving, supportive, understanding, and as patient as you possibly can be. Never forget there is hope, even when it seems hopeless.

The hardest part of my loss was coming to terms with the permanency and the fact that's all there was. All the time I got to spend with my sister and nieces was all the time I would have. I'm still working on that part, because it's just too overwhelming to fully realize it. It was also difficult losing contact with friends and acquaintances just because they couldn't talk to me anymore ... they didn't know what to say.

*

ALEXIS VON UTTER
Alexis was 12 when her father Marc
died at age 57 from lung cancer complications

The hardest part for me was going through and seeing my dad's stuff all over the house, and also acting at school like everything is normal. I didn't overcome it until about three years later, but I also never let myself come to the realization and accept what was happening. I overcame it because I decided that instead of wallowing in self-pity, I was going to make my dad proud by growing up and being the daughter he would have been proud to see grow up.

*

HEATHER WALLACE-REY
Heather was 40 when her father John
died suddenly at age 71 of a massive heart attack

The hardest part of my loss was learning how to be myself again; maybe even learning to be a better person than I was before. It was also very hard to know that there are people who liked the version of me before my dad died better than the version of me who exists today.

*

DIANNE WEST
Dianne's 69-year-old husband Vern
died from multiple myeloma in 2010

I found myself alone for the first time in my life, and it was frightening. While I had been handling most everything during the previous cancer years, the reality of having to live the rest of my life without Vern was devastating. I felt I needed to act normal during the workweek, to be the "old" Dianne everyone expected me to be; but this behavior took a lot of energy and caused me to crash hard on the weekends. My mother-in-law was widowed for thirty years, and my mother was widowed for fourteen years, yet I don't recall ever having any conversations with them about what it was like or how I might be able to help. I'm rather amazed at that now that I am widowed myself – and I wish they were here so we could talk. I guess we don't know until we know and then everything changes. Death isn't handled well here in North America. People seem to think it won't happen to them. They don't want to talk about it. They aren't comfortable dealing with those who are grieving. They just want us to get back to how we used to be.

216

Unfortunately, that is not an option. If you're reading this book, then I congratulate you for taking an important step to learn how to help your bereaved friends and relatives. Please share your new-found knowledge with others.

I have reached the five-year milestone, and yet I still miss my husband. Every. Single. Day. I am fully living my life ... traveling, learning, volunteering, experiencing new things. Trying to do good things that will honor him, but still missing the life he and I should be living right now.

My grief is still present, and it's important that you understand that. It doesn't magically go away at any particular point. Time can soften the edges of our grief, but it remains, ready to pull us back down in an instant. Stand by your bereaved friends. Stand with them. Acknowledge their grief. Embrace their sadness. Love them. Our hearts are broken and fragile, but your love and friendship can be a critical lifeline. Be present, be loving, be understanding, be generous with your time . . . and you will be blessed.

*

She who heals herself heals others.
LYNDA CHELDELIN FELL

CHAPTER THIRTEEN

OUR JOURNEY

The journey of a thousand miles
begins with one step.
LAO TZU

The writers in this book come from many different places, backgrounds and beliefs. Because each journey through loss is unique, and to help you better understand their insight, it's fair for you to know the shoes they walk in. If you wish to skip this chapter because it is too hard to read, do not feel bad. We understand, truly we do. But please feel free to return to this chapter at any point to enrich your own understanding.

The best vision is insight.
MALCOLM FORBES

Thoughtful Insight

*

EMILY BAIRD-LEVINE
Emily's 43-year-old brother Don
died from a heart attack in 2004

My brother Don, of blessed memory, was a very lovable, funny, giving, intelligent person. He was truly a *mensch* (Yiddish for someone of consequence; someone to admire and emulate; an upright, honorable, decent person. Or, as a rabbi of ours once said, "A mensch is someone who does the right thing, at the right time, for the right reason.") This sums up Don very well. Don was the valedictorian of his high school graduating class. He earned his B.A. in Economics from Pomona College, and worked as an acquisitions analyst for a company that managed investments for low income housing projects.

Don was diagnosed with type I diabetes at age three. This was at a time when glucometers to test blood sugar did not exist. Blood sugar was tested with urine tests that indicated what one's blood sugar was twenty-four hours prior. I believe Don was around seventeen or eighteen when he started to complain about his eyesight. My mom took both of us to the eye doctor, who discovered that Don had diabetic retinopathy, along with other complications from the diabetes. He was immediately admitted to the hospital. His kidneys were failing, he was put on dialysis, and his insulin intake needed to be managed.

Don was in and out the hospital for an extended amount of time during his senior year of high school. He went for dialysis several times a week. He did start college, and had to drop out for a year to have a kidney transplant. My oldest brother, Andy, donated a kidney to Don. This kidney gave Don an extra twenty-four years of life that he wouldn't otherwise have had.

Don was put on prednisone after that transplant. This is necessary because it is used as an anti-rejection medication. Unfortunately, steroids are very difficult on internal organs and on blood sugar. Don was able to manage his blood sugar while taking prednisone, but over time the effects of the steroids took a toll on his lungs specifically. He would get sick often, and a few days before he passed away, he was doing breathing treatments, but they weren't helping. Don ultimately lost too much oxygen, and had a heart attack. Between the damage to his brain and the heart attack, he didn't make it. He was forty-three.

*

EMILY BARNHARDT
Emily's 20-year-old friend/roommate
Hannah died by suicide in 2014

Hannah, my best friend and roommate, was the type of person who changed a room's atmosphere, making it suddenly more vibrant and exciting. She was the type of person you know you can count on, the type of person who makes you feel deeply loved, and the type of whose energy and laugh are contagious. Hannah embodied confidence and joy. What most people didn't know, however, was how much she struggled with insecurity – over her potential, her personality, her worth, her relationships and her future. I never understood why she felt so self-conscious; she was such a lovable, smart, fun and valuable girl. I'll never be able to understand exactly how it felt to be in her head, but from talks we had, I knew she was struggling to feel hopeful about her ability to overcome the internal battles in her mind and to succeed at all the dreams she had for her life.

Hannah was going through a particularly rough patch when she took her life. One evening, she came home crying and told me she'd been fired from the job that she loved. Other events of that weekend had been extremely tough as well. Two days later, I was at a restaurant when I got a call from Hannah's mother, who lives in a different state. She was concerned about Hannah's well-being, and asked if I had talked to Hannah that day. I hadn't been home and hadn't talked to her, so I got off the phone with her mom and called her. Hannah was crying and obviously in distress when she answered, so I told her that we would meet up, and I would help her get through what was going on. I needed to close my check at the restaurant, so I got off the phone with Hannah, telling her I'd call her right back to figure out where we should meet. However, when I called back shortly after, she didn't answer. You know that bad feeling you get in your gut sometimes? I felt that feeling, so I went looking for her. I drove around for hours, looking everywhere I could think of, but had no luck. When it got late and I ran out of ideas, I returned to our apartment for the night. I had hoped Hannah had fallen asleep at a coworker's house or some similar type of situation.

That next morning, Hannah's mother called me at 8 a.m. to tell me that Hannah had taken her life just after she and I had spoken on the phone the night before. The police contacted her parents shortly after they found her.

I've stood on wobbly feet the past year, looking at a new chapter I wasn't prepared for and didn't want, trying to figure out exactly how it has changed me, and how to find solid ground again. I've grappled with the concept of "closure," and wondered if it's even possible. Experiencing this level of grief itself has changed me forever. I've learned that grief isn't a coat you put on and then take off once you feel warm again. In a way, you have to absorb grief. It's been a process of acceptance and change and adjustment for me. It has become a part of me, not in a sense that it is my identity, but in a sense that it has redefined the person I am.

*

CHRISTINE BASTONE
Christine's sister Elizabeth
died in 2012 at age 38

On February 11, 2012, I was reading my Kindle, blissfully

unaware that my youngest sister Liz died by suicide the day before. I knew she had been unhappy, but I had absolutely no idea that she was suicidal. I kept meaning to reach out to her at least one more time to try and find out what was going on. I knew something was wrong because of her behavior a few months previously when Liz had come for a visit. But sadly, I ran out of time.

My parents called shortly after eight in the evening to give me the sad news. I was in shock. I had never been so shocked by anything in my life! I started aimlessly walking around the kitchen and living room area. I sat down. I stood back up. My mouth dropped open. I put my hands on my head. I simply could not believe what I had just heard.

My sister's death has changed my life. It has made me a little more outspoken. It caused me to question everything I was ever taught to believe, and has changed those beliefs a little. It has made me extremely sensitive to the way we talk about suicide, and how it is portrayed on TV shows and in the movies.

*

ERICA GALE BELTZ
Erica's 5-year-old son Luke Jordan died in 2002
from a fallen banister in his aunt's driveway

Luke lived his whole life in five years, and God was present the last couple of days Luke was here. He was "star student" in his kindergarten class that week, and we went to my sister's house to work on Luke's "All About Me" poster. My teenage niece, Ashley, had just returned from the store with supplies for the poster when Luke went running outside to greet her, bursting with excitement to get started on his poster. Just then, a heavy wooden banister gave way, falling onto Luke. Despite the valiant efforts of many, Luke died from the crushing impact. Time stopped for me that day.

My grief group and The Compassionate Friends were such sources of healing. I am not proud to say that I am a better person now because of Luke's passing, but his life really made an impact on me, and continues to fill my heart. I have had many great losses since Luke's passing. My Uncle Jay and I were close, and he was diagnosed with brain cancer and the outlook was gloom. He lived for five years and fought a valiant fight. We knew he was on precious borrowed time, and it was like holding hands with the other side. When Jay died, we really wept and still do. When my Grandma Norma passed away, I watched my mom and her sisters say goodbye to their sweet mama. I was able to support Mom just as she had always done for me. I was inspired by the bereaved families, who were able to minister to those just starting to face this journey. I now have my own ministry, and it truly helps me to do something that will help others, and to honor Luke as well. The friendships that I have gained will always be with me.

*

SOPHIA BLOWERS
Sophia was 50 when her mother Amy
died at age 79 of internal bleeding

The most dramatic loss I have experienced was the loss of my mother due to internal bleeding; however, every loss has had a profound impact on my life. I lost my first pregnancy while entering the second trimester. I lost my dad to a slow and nasty cancer. They each changed me and reshaped my life. Any loss has an effect on your life, some are more pronounced and some are more subtle. The loss of my dad was expected. There was a larger support group surrounding him, and more time to say and do what was necessary. The loss of my baby was unexpected, but I was told it was not a big deal because I was so early in the pregnancy. I saw my baby, recognized its form, but was supposed to pretend it was just a mass of tissue; after all, I was nineteen and unmarried. I should be grateful. The loss of my mom was a long, drawn-out affair, but her death itself was unexpected. The reason I feel that this was the most life-altering loss was because of the complexity of the loss. It was not a peaceful passing. I hate myself for some of the

225

things I did. I excuse it by saying that I thought I was saving my mom's life and doing what the doctors said, but it does not change the fact that I participated in the pain and fear my mom felt before she died. No amount of self-talk takes away the pictures that are on a constant loop when I close my eyes.

*

LYNDA CHELDELIN FELL
Lynda's 15-year-old daughter Aly
died in a car accident in 2009

On August 5, 2009, we got the phone call every parent dreads: our fifteen year-old daughter, Aly, had been in a car accident. A straight-A student and year-round competitive swimmer, Aly and a handful of senior swimmers traveled to Seattle to watch Michael Phelps compete in the U.S. Open. After a long eighteen-hour day, late at night on an unfamiliar road, the driver of Aly's car missed a stop sign at a dark intersection. A father coming home from work in his truck hit the rear passenger door at fifty-five miles an hour, right where our daughter was sitting. She died instantly. Life as we knew it ended, and a new one taking us through hell was just beginning.

But there is a silver lining in my journey: the creation of the Grief Diaries village dedicated to comforting those who don't have the abundance of support that I was blessed with.

I would exchange it all in a heartbeat to go back in time, but that isn't to be. So I am very grateful that God put me on the path to help people share their stories. I find great comfort in knowing that moments are fleeting, memories are permanent and love is forever.

*

MICHELLE DETWILER
Michelle's 19-year-old daughter Emily
died in 2014 due to congenital complications

After giving birth to a son with medical challenges, my husband and I chose to provide foster care for medically fragile babies for the state of Washington. Emily was adopted into our family through that program, joining us when she was released from the hospital at six months of age. We were told that Emily would not live very long. We poured our life and love into that fragile baby, and she grew into a beautiful teen, despite her many medical challenges.

At age seventeen, Emily had surgery to correct lifelong problems with her bowels. The surgery was performed, but it didn't heal correctly. It split apart, and the day before her planned discharge home, Emily needed emergency surgery to repair her bowel. When Emily came home from the hospital, she was not the same as she had been earlier in her life. Where there once was a smiling young lady sitting in her wheelchair, we now had a tired daughter who needed nutrition infused into her veins through an IV pump, because her bowels still did not work. I think we knew at that time it was the beginning of the end.

Emily's health continued to waver for a year after that surgery, and then she began to decline. One Saturday, Emily was breathing erratically, and I knew it was going to be her last weekend, maybe even her last day, with us. Our family and two close friends joined us, along with Emily's two favorite nurses. The nursing shift change was happening, and when hospice arrived they both stayed to get the new orders from hospice. My husband had gone to the train station to pick up Grandma. Our older sons came to visit their sister as she lay quietly in bed. The television played her favorite cartoon movies, and her brothers sat telling her about the exciting parts that she had always enjoyed. As her breathing slowed and her heart monitor began to alarm, we decided to just turn it off. My husband had not returned with Grandma yet, and I was beginning to worry that Emily would die before they arrived. We encouraged Emily for more vigorous breaths with, "Grandma's coming! Grandma's coming!" And she made it, staying alive till my mother and husband arrived. One of the nurses ran to the driveway, and told them to forget the luggage and just come into the house. Grandma sat by Emily's bedside and chatted with her for a few minutes, while I whispered in Emily's other ear to go with Jesus when she saw him. I wanted to reassure her that it was okay, that we would be okay, and she could go.

Grandma said, "Well, Emily, it looks like you are getting tired now so I'll let you go to sleep. Good night, Emily, we'll see you in the morning." Dad sat down next to Emily, and held her hand. He whispered sweetness to her, as our family stood around. Emily took her last breath, and then she moved on to heaven. I could never imagine losing a part of my heart, and yet it happened. There is nothing that can compare to the loss of a child. My vision now is to be able to give some measure of hope back to families who are grieving and in the same spot I'm in.

*

CHRISTINE DUMINIAK
Christine's 86-year-old mother Ann
died from an aortic aneurysm in 2004

My mother, Ann Rugel, was the life force in our family, and boy did she enjoy life! She loved dancing with my father, and they had won many jitterbug contests together in their younger years. She immensely enjoyed their mixed bowling league, playing Rummy Cube, Scrabble, Pinochle, coupon-collecting, trips to casinos with the senior citizens, traveling, and socializing with her friends and strangers. She loved big band music and especially Frank Sinatra. My mother refused to look and "get old," as she would often say. She was quite the fashionista, and enjoyed smartly dressing up and wearing jeweled high-heel shoes, even into her eighties! Most of all, she loved being with her family.

Around 2002, at age eighty-four, my mother was diagnosed with a huge nine centimeter abdominal aortic aneurysm. Doctors were so alarmed that they wanted to perform an operation immediately to remove it before it could burst and kill her. My mother's jaw-dropping reply to the shocked doctors was, "No, I can't. I have to go bowling today!" Another reason she declined to have the surgery was because she felt like this was really a good way to die. She believed it would be quick and that she would have very little pain. So she put herself in God's hands for the timing on this.

Another factor in my mom's refusal for the surgery was that my dad had passed in 2000, and my mother often talked about wanting to be with him. She understandably, of course, missed her loving husband of fifty-seven years, and was very lonely without him. Then, on February 29, 2004, and just days before her eighty-sixth birthday, my mother got her wish. She was called Home very quickly due to the sudden rupturing of her aneurysm while she was staying in the hospital for a different health issue. Even though this shouldn't have come as a shock, it still was to my sisters and me and our families. Words cannot express the deep pain of grief I felt in my chest. The only time I felt light-hearted was when my sisters and I would meet up every Saturday to clean out my parents' house. When the three of us were all together, it was a bittersweet trip down memory lane.

The hardest part for me was not being able to talk to and do certain activities with my loved one. So even though at first I did not have the enthusiastic desire to participate in these same activities with other people, I thought I would give it a try anyway. This way I would still be participating in an activity I used to enjoy, so the loss would not be a double one.

*

SHARON EHLERS
Sharon's best friend Joy died in 2009 at age 52
Sharon's former fiancé John died in 2012 at age 59

I met Joy the early 1990s. Our friendship evolved from being coworkers into being great friends. Joy was one of the most thoughtful people I knew. As we spent more time together, I also noticed that there was also a lot of pain in her life. Over the course of the next ten to fifteen years, Joy was on a rollercoaster of emotions, and tried to take her own life numerous times. On a Sunday evening in 2009, her husband called to tell me she had died by suicide. I felt like life had been sucked right out of me; I collapsed on the floor. I had lost my best friend. Someone I spoke to every day. How are you supposed to move forward after this? The only way was to allow my grief to jump to the forefront.

Just over two years after Joy died, I found out my former fiancé, John, also took his own life. He was the love of my life. My soul mate. My other half. He was kind and funny. He "got" me. He made me happy. We had known each other for many years before we fell in love. When it hit, it was magical. We started on a road where we laughed, cried, and faced many ups and downs. When you know you want to be with someone forever, you work to make it happen. We bought a townhouse, and got engaged. Life together was good. Over time, the anger over his divorce started to consume him. It affected our relationship to the point that he became someone I really didn't know anymore. In 2009, he went his way and I went mine. I was heartbroken and devastated. Even though I knew it was for the best, I never really stopped loving him. In 2012, on a beautiful sunny April day, my sister told me John had died by suicide. I am not sure it registered. It broke my heart and soul into a trillion pieces. I was filled with extreme sadness and heartache, and it hasn't gone away.

*

ANNAH ELIZABETH
Annah's newborn son Gavin Michael
died 26 minutes following his birth

I recall three distinct, childhood memories: I wanted to change the world, to end hate, injustice and suffering. I dreamed of being a writer. I wanted one day to be a mom, but not an old mom, so I was going to have those babies before I turned thirty. I never believed in fate or destiny, and then a man came to fix the broken lock on my front door, and my life was forever changed. That handyman and I quickly became friends. Nearly four months later, we went out on our first date, and four years after that we were newly married and expecting our first child. I was twenty-six years old, and life was rolling along right according to my master plan. That pregnancy progressed without so much as a hiccup, and I worked right up until the day before I delivered.

On May 11, 1990, my labor progressed exactly as all the books said it would but shortly after the nurse hooked me up to the monitors, all of that changed. An emergency Cesarean section later, doctors discovered that my son had aspirated on his meconium, the baby's first stool. While Warren sat in the waiting room and I lay asleep under anesthesia, a medical team worked to save my son's life. Unable to overcome his circumstances, Gavin Michael died twenty-six minutes after he entered this world.

*

DAPHNE GREER
Daphne's 5-year-old daughter Lydia
died in a car accident in 2008

It was a beautiful midsummer morning. The sun was peeking brightly over the tree tops as we drove down the highway. The fresh smell of summer was in the air. We had made this daily commute for years, the same stretch of twenty-mile highway en route to day care and my work. I enjoyed this time with the

231

children, listening to their entertaining stories, questions about life, and hearing their sibling banter in the back seat. They would often hold hands, sing or draw, and color to pass the time. But on this beautiful midsummer morning, just a few short miles from our home, we were involved in a two-vehicle accident. My five-year-old daughter, Lydia, passed away as a result. My son and I had minor injuries.

My journey has been anything but easy. In the seven years since the accident, it has been difficult, challenging, immensely painful, yet all the while full of amazement and awe. I have changed both inside and out, and my passions and views on life have turned, making me appreciate every day I have been given.

*

BRENDA KLEINSASSER
Brenda's 88 year-old mother
died from congestive heart failure in 2011

I lost my beloved mother, who was my best friend, on May 31, 2011. She had been in a nursing home since February because of congestive heart failure. She was on oxygen to help her breathe more easily. It was hard to see my mother this way. She had always been such a strong person; she was eighty-eight years old, but was still driving her car. The last morning that she drove me to work was when this whole nightmare began. I came out of the clinic that evening to find her sitting in the driver's seat of her neighbor's car. She had had some kind of attack during the day, and went for help. She was to have a thoracentesis at the end of the week to remove fluid from behind her lung. The morning of the test, she was having difficulty breathing and I called 9-1-1. That was the beginning of the final chapter of my mother's life. She went to the hospital, and was transferred to the nursing home five days later. In less than four months, she was gone. I had lost my best friend.

*

DEANA MARTIN
Deana's only two children, 25-year-old Amanda
and 21-year-old Logan, died in a car accident in 2011

On January 18, 2011, my children's stepmother died. We lived in Georgia, and my children made plans to drive to Indiana for the funeral. My daughter's fiancé agreed to drive them. My three-year-old granddaughter was also in tow. The drive went fine, and they made it to Indiana with no problems. At 11 a.m. on the morning of their stepmother's funeral, I was returning to my desk from a routine meeting with my boss. I noticed my cellphone had many missed calls from area code 317. I knew that whoever called had tried desperately to reach me; I must have had twenty missed calls. It turns out that there had been a terrible accident, and both of my children were dead.

It had been snowing heavily, and just a mile down the road on their way to the funeral home, my daughter's car hit a patch of black ice, and spun into the path of a semi-truck, which hit their car. The impact from the semi pushed the car down into a ravine where it crashed into a tree. As I sat there in a daze, the rescue team was still trying to cut my children out of the mangled car. My children died on January 20, 2011, at 9:58 a.m. From that point forward, everything became a blur. I remember thinking, "How am I going to do this?" It was similar to that first childbirth experience, when you think "How am I going to do this?" You don't have a clue but you are led innately.

*

DIANE MCKENZIE-SAPP
Diane's 65-year-old husband Ron
died from renal failure in 2006

I was the beauty queen, the "Miss Congeniality" type, and didn't see marriage in my future. I had seen the movie The Stepford Wives, and wasn't about to stifle my individuality. What if I found a partner who would make me a better person as if he was my other half, melding together like oil and vinegar making a great dressing? Nah, what were the odds of that? I decided to become a stewardess and travel the world.

Along came Ron. Ron was the popular kid from the poor side of the tracks. He loved the Baltimore Colts, hanging out with his guy friends, rock and roll music, his car and playing baseball. He was the best shortstop that never played. Ron had to work to finish high school. No one in his family had ever finished high school. I went to Catholic school and played varsity field hockey, basketball and softball. Ron saw the good in people, he was optimistic, always had a smile on his face. I was an opportunist and liked dogs more than people. Ron did everything because it was the right thing to do. I had always calculated the risk versus benefit of my actions. Ron was oil to my vinegar. By our second date I knew Ron would be the father of my children.

Fast forward to May 1997, when Ron was diagnosed with colon cancer. A fresh grad out of college removed Ron's cancer and bowel on the left side and, with the same cancer-infected instrument, pierced Ron's right kidney. In 2006, Ron's cancer had spread to his bones and his liver was three times the normal size. Ron chose to stop dialysis, and opted for a renal failure death over colon cancer. He died in hospice. As a hospice nurse, I should have been okay. I didn't know that I would die that day as well. There was the constant grayness, the tears and my broken heart. The pain of grief is real, like the phantom pain of amputees. My heart bled tears. Everything that was good was gone. I felt incomplete, broken, and had no reason to welcome tomorrow. Tornadoes, earthquakes, and volcanos leave the destruction I felt in my soul. My words, "I'm fine," belied the woman inside. She was lost without her other half, melting away, broken, and fading into nothingness with each passing day. I had lost my partner, my future and myself.

*

JULIE MJELVE
Julie's 42-year-old husband Cameron
died by suicide in 2011

I met James Cameron Mjelve in 2005 while we were both living in Edmonton. At the time he worked for a laborer's union. We married in 2007, and had three beautiful children together: one boy and two girls. In 2009, my husband returned to university. In 2010, his second year, he seemed to have more difficulty maintaining the work and scheduling of his courses. Over the Christmas break, he seemed different, a bit off from his usual self. Perhaps a little depressed, but nothing that raised any immediate concern. I chalked this up to stresses of university. On January 31, 2011, my youngest daughter was born with the diagnosis of Down syndrome. Essentially, adding one more stressors to his life, turned out to be more than he was able to cope with. On the evening of July 21, 2011, the police rang my doorbell. They informed me that my husband had committed suicide. My life has changed dramatically since that time. It has been very difficult to raise three children on my own. At the time my husband passed away, they were three and a half years old, two years old and five months old. There has been a tremendous amount of stress trying to cope with not only the traumatic nature of his death, but trying to help three very small children understand death and grieving, somehow still finding a way to grieve myself, and also the pressures of daily living, all at the same time.

*

MARY POTTER KENYON
Mary's 60-year-old husband David
died of heart failure in 2012

My father died in 1986. My mother died in November 2010, on my fifty-first birthday. My husband David, a five-year cancer survivor, died of heart failure in March 2012. My eight year old grandson Jacob lost a three-year battle with cancer in August 2013.

235

The morning after my husband David unexpectedly passed away, I sat down with a journal, and filled three pages with words of thanks for the bonus five and a half years we shared after his cancer treatment; the life insurance policy that had been reinstated just twenty-seven days previously that allowed me to bury him, purchase a vehicle, and not worry about money for nearly eighteen months; and the family that surrounded me like cotton batting. I instinctively knew what I needed, even if I wasn't sure how to get it. I wanted prayer, and I needed God's Word. My journey in the ensuing months was as much about faith as it was about grief. It seemed that my extreme loss literally brought me to my knees.

*

NANCY REDMOND
Nancy's 40-year-old husband Kevin
died of a heart attack in 2012

On May 10, 2012, a beautiful spring morning, I lost my husband, best friend and soulmate to a massive heart attack. Kevin passed in his work truck and was finally found fourteen hours later. The medical examiner and the funeral director advised against viewing Kevin's remains. I never got to see Kevin again, and I feel that's partly responsible for my difficulty in dealing with this loss. He touched my leg to let me know he was leaving for work that morning, kissed me goodbye like he'd never see me again (he was right!), hugged me tight, but never came home. I was blessed to spend the best ten years of my life with this incredible man who completed my heart and soul.

In some ways, I truly feel that God spared me the pain of watching the love of my life deal with a terminal illness. However, we did find out at the time of the autopsy that Kevin also had an extremely advanced form of melanoma that had gone untreated and had probably metastasized. I send out my love to those heroes who lovingly and unselfishly care for their loves through illness that so viciously rips them from our lives.

*

MARYELLEN ROACH
MaryEllen's sister Suzette and two nieces, 6-year-old
Vivian and 8-year-old Lillian, died in car accident in 2012

In 2007, my sister, Suzette and her two girls, Lillian and Vivian, moved in with my parents, and everyone was thrilled. Vivian could be with the grandpa she adored ALL the time, and Lillian loved being with her grandparents and living in the country. Lillian and Vivian balanced each other out, played well together and were best friends. They were my sister's children, but they really were the entire family's kids.

Lillian was one of the most popular kids in school. Even kids who were much older than Lillian knew who she was. She became a legend for being an advanced reader: Lillian was tested for reading comprehension in the second grade, and she scored with a twelfth grade reading level, the highest the grading went. Vivian started kindergarten when she was five. Although more reserved and modest than her older sister, Vivian was also highly intelligent and popular. But everything changed on July 26, 2012.

That night around 11 p.m., my mom called asking if Suzette and the girls had stopped by my house. Suzette wasn't answering her phone, which was unusual, and they should have been home hours earlier. Suzette was always good about letting everyone know if she would be later than expected, but neither of us had heard from her. Mom said she was going to call Suzette again, and would let me know when she got in touch with her. When mom called back forty-five minutes later, I thought she was calling to tell me Suzette and the girls had arrived home, but when I heard the tone in her voice, I knew. Although I wish I could forget the words she said, but I doubt I ever will.

"MaryEllen. The sheriff is here. Suzette and the girls were in an accident." My mind began racing, when Mom said, "and they're all dead." When I heard those words, I felt a separation happen. It felt like I was looking down at myself, seeing myself talking on the phone; I went completely numb, and my voice sounded muffled. I thought, "No, it's not possible. They made a mistake. No... that... couldn't... have happened!" Sadly, it wasn't a mistake. Nearly half of my family was gone just like that. The life I had was gone, and I was shattered into a million pieces. I died, and was reborn a different person the day they moved to Heaven. It has been three years, and it's still beyond comprehension that this happened to our close little family.

*

MARY LEE ROBINSON
Mary Lee's 63-year-old husband Pat
died of a sudden cerebral hemorrhage in 2013

My husband, Pat, and I had very recently relocated to our dream retirement destination of Myrtle Beach, South Carolina. Pat had suffered an aneurysm in his carotid artery a year and a half before we met, and then had a mini stroke in West Virginia. Medically, we thought it was resolved, and Pat appeared to be the picture of health. One afternoon, Pat happily waved, and walked out the door to go play pool with his buddies. He was an excellent player, and it was his favorite thing in the world. He never came home again. He had a stroke in the pool hall, and was rushed to the emergency room. When I arrived at the hospital, his neurosurgeon gave me the very bad news that Pat would not survive. The best that could be hoped for was that he would be in a vegetative state permanently. With no family or friends around, I had the very tough decision to remove my husband from life support. Since we'd talked about it many, many times while caring for our elders, and had prepared the legal documents, I knew with certainty what I must do. It was devastating. Five days later Pat was gone. The loss knocked me off my pins, utterly.

*

KRISTI SMITH
Kristi's 48-year-old husband Michael
died from cardiac arrest in 2011

Mike was hardwired to be the center of activity, so he channeled that energy, and used it everywhere he went. He used it most powerfully in his role as an involvement pastor. His passion and enthusiasm to serve God, as you can imagine, dramatically changed the climate at church. Mike was truly the best dad I have ever known. He loved our girls, and they adored their dad. He read to them, played games with them, and taught them everything that he knew. The best thing he taught our girls was how they should expect a man to treat them by watching how he treated me as his wife. He called me his bride until the day that he died. Most important, Mike showed the girls what a father's love should look like, and pointed to God as their father. Grace was not just something spoken at the dinner table; grace was his way of life.

At the age of forty-eight, Mike died suddenly and without any warning. It happened one evening in October, while riding back from a meeting with a friend. They were almost to our house, when Mike said he felt tired, and leaned his head over to rest. He never woke up. Arriving in our driveway less than a minute later, Mike's buddy was not able to wake Mike up, and that's when we got the dreaded knock on the door. His friend was in a panic because he could not wake Mike up, and he was afraid something was seriously wrong. Chaos ensued as the girls and I ran out to the car to see what was happening. I could tell Mike did not look right, so I sent the girls, ages fifteen and seventeen, to get the doctor who lived three doors down from us, and to find someone to call 9-1-1. His friend and I got Mike out of the car just in time for the doctor to start CPR, but Mike just lay there. Pale. Too pale. Ten minutes later, the paramedics arrived. The girls and I grabbed our shoes and drove silently with Mike's friend to the hospital. Almost an hour later, when the doctor came and told us that Mike had died, it was like the wind got knocked out of us. The girls and I were heartbroken; literally shredded emotionally. The whole town, our church, our families and friends were as shocked as we were. Mike was the most alive man we had ever known, and now he was dead. That was four years ago. Sometimes it feels like a lifetime ago, and sometimes it feels like last night. Everything has changed since then. Everything.

Despite my loss, love lives on.

*

ALEXIS VON UTTER
Alexis was 12 when her father Marc
died at age 57 from lung cancer complications

My dad was the main caretaker at my home. He drove me everywhere, taught me how to play the sports I do now, taught me all of the homework, helped me with my art and school projects, and taught me how to cook simple things. My dad was everyone's favorite person. He was kind, funny, an amazing cook and smart. He was the best person to be around because he was happy. Everyone loved coming over to spend time with him and hear his jokes, along with a little salsa and guacamole on the side.

In May 2011, my dad had to have shoulder surgery. As he started healing in late August, his lower back started to hurt. It got to a point where he couldn't even get up by himself. My mom took him to the hospital, and he wasn't getting much better, but they couldn't figure out what was wrong. My dad was flown over to Georgetown Hospital in Washington, D.C. We went to visit Dad and found out he had stage four lung cancer. Dad had a respirator in his throat, and couldn't talk. My mom had taken time off from work, but my brother just acted like nothing was really happening. I was falling apart, but my dad was staying strong.

On December 4, 2011, I had to say goodbye. Dad hadn't been able to move and he was blown up from the medicine. I later found out that a natural antibody designed to attack the cancer was instead attacking Dad's nervous system. There was nothing anyone could do. I had to say goodbye to my best friend and my dad. My dad was strong, and let out few tears, but he kept going for my family. At around 7:10 p.m., they took Dad off the life support and let him fall asleep. At 7:20 p.m., my father passed away.

My mom had to become two people, and take care of us. I have had to have a nanny ever since. That day ruined my life, but also helped me to learn so much more. To this day I can remember all the good times. But I will also never forget the horrible sadness on my dad's face when he realized he had to say goodbye.

*

HEATHER WALLACE-REY
Heather was 40 when her father John
died suddenly at age 71 of a massive heart attack

In April 2012, my dad was stolen from us. My father, probably one of the most physically fit seventy-one-year-old men you would ever meet, who spent his time running, biking and going to the dojo, suffered a massive heart attack and passed away.

My dad died the same way he lived: on his own terms. At about 6:30 a.m. on the day he died, he told a man in his apartment complex that he wasn't feeling very well. Ten hours later, the pain was bad enough that my dad took the elevator down from his condo to the management office, and asked the woman in the office to call an ambulance. She was the last person to have a conversation with him. My dad arrived at the hospital and, after numerous attempts to resuscitate him, we were told there was no hope. In a matter of four hours he had been rushed to the hospital, we had arrived at the hospital, he was there, he was gone, and we were on the way home with his personal affects, which included some random vials of ibuprofen, two sticks of lip balm, glasses, a Swiss army knife, a package of Kleenex, two keychains, a handheld game, a case with his hearing aid batteries, two books (one about tai chi), his sandals and socks, and a Shotokan karate jacket. I felt as if I was lovingly carrying the final possessions of MacGyver. Far be it for my dad to either wear his sandals without socks OR to not come prepared to a heart attack. This wonderful man who had taught us to "keep your winter gloves in the car, in case the car breaks down" and to "never let the gas tank get down to less than a quarter of a tank" was certainly not going to be caught unprepared.

Ironically enough, I know he certainly was not prepared for a heart attack at that moment, because he still had two unopened half gallons of "the good ice cream" in his freezer when he died. Those two half gallons would definitely have been opened and eaten if he had known he wasn't coming back for them.

*

DIANNE WEST
Dianne's 69-year-old husband Vern
died from multiple myeloma in 2010

One magical moment in the summer of 1969 changed my life forever. A chance meeting. A spark. A love that was meant to be. A love that defined me. A love I will carry with me forever.

In 1964, my husband arrived as a first year teacher and basketball coach at my high school. I arrived there as an eighth grade student. No one – especially us – would have ever guessed that five years later we would fall in love and marry. We were blessed with a son in 1976. In 1982, we moved to Las Vegas and, after a year of coaching, Vern went to work at UNLV's sports arena. After twenty years, he retired to open the Orleans Arena. Vern was an amazing teacher, fabulous coach and inspiring mentor to many.

Vern had always had back issues that flared from time to time, so we weren't initially alarmed when the pain began in 2006. However, when he got to the point where he could hardly walk, I convinced him to see a doctor. A CT scan was done but didn't show anything, so Vern was sent to a physical therapist. And he got worse. We finally begged his primary physician to get insurance approval for an MRI. We weren't home too long after the procedure when the doctor called and said, "My God, man, you have a tumor on your spine." I don't think I'll ever forget those words. We met with the surgeon early the next morning. A small room. Vern in a wheelchair, me on a stool, the doctor showing us the MRI scans. The tumor. The hot spots. Spinal compression fractures. And so many lytic lesions. Multiple myeloma. Cancer. Metastasized. Not a good prognosis.

And so it began, four plus years. Surgeries. Mistakes. Rehab. Physical therapy. Infections. GI bleeds. Pleural effusions. Pneumonia. Pulmonary embolism. Chemo. Radiation. So very many blood transfusions. Colostomy. Kidney failure. Dialysis. He went through so much. And then there was nothing more they could do to him. For him.

Vern's final days were spent at Nathan Adelson Hospice. No more pricks and prods or waking him up for rounds. He was peaceful. I stayed with him twenty-four hours a day. And those final four days were a gift. He spoke very little the first two days and then was silent, but I have no doubt at all that he was able to hear my words. When the death rattle arrived, I gently slid into his hospital bed, held him close and spoke to him, until he slipped away hours later.

*

HOW TO HELP THE NEWLY BEREAVED

Heavy hearts, like heavy clouds in the sky,
are best relieved by the letting go of a little water.
ANTOINE RIVAROL

CHAPTER FOURTEEN

MEET THE WRITERS

*

EMILY BAIRD-LEVINE
Emily's 43-year-old brother Don
died from a heart attack in 2004
ejbairdlevine@gmail.com

Emily Baird-Levine was born in
Los Angeles, California, and raised
in a small city in the San Gabriel
Valley. She is the youngest of four
children. She earned her B.A.
degree in psychology at UC Santa
Cruz and her master's degree in
social work from San Diego State
University.

She met her husband, Bob, while
they both worked as child
protective service social workers in
Santa Clara, California. She and
Bob moved to Arizona right after
getting married, and had both their
children there. Emily and family
have lived in the Pacific Northwest
for almost fifteen years. She has
been a stay-at-home mom for over
twenty years.

*
EMILY BARNHARDT
Emily's friend and roommate Hannah died in 2014 at age 20
changethatlasts90@gmail.com http://changethatlasts.weebly.com

Emily Barnhardt was born and raised in Charlotte, North Carolina, where she lived with her parents and two siblings until age sixteen. She then attended boarding school in Asheville, North Carolina, for the remainder of high school. Emily began her undergraduate studies at the University of Denver in Colorado, dual-majoring in Business and in Hospitality Management. After her first two years of college, Emily endured many challenging circumstances in her personal life, and relocated to Boca Raton, Florida, at the age of twenty-two. Through the trials she experienced in life, Emily developed deep concern and empathy for people who were hurting, and realized her calling in life is helping others. She returned to college at Florida Atlantic University to pursue a master's

degree in Social Work. She was awarded the AlyBlue Media Humanitarian Award 2015 for her extraordinary contribution to raising suicide awareness at a young age. Emily finds strength, freedom, and restoration in her Christian faith, and contributes the healing and change in her life to the Lord. One year after her loss, she decided to move back home to Charlotte. She is currently working and continuing her degree in social work.

*
CHRISTINE BASTONE
Christine's 38-year-old sister Liz
died by suicide in 2012
C.Bastone@mail.com * www.facebook.com/CricketsPlace1

Christine Bastone is a stay-at-home mom in her forties who has only recently figured out that she wants to be a writer when she grows up! She was born in northeast Ohio and moved to Florida in May 1995. She married Angelo Bastone in July 1997. They have a son, Joshua, born in 2001 and a daughter, Katelyn, born in 2004. The four of them live together in their house at the end of a quiet street in central Florida. Christine has always loved to read, and was thrilled when her husband gave her a Kindle for Christmas in 2011. She has since read hundreds of Kindle books.

Christine is an award-winning writer of *Grief Diaries: Surviving Loss by Suicide*, co-author of *Grief Diaries: Surviving Loss of a Sibling*, and contributed to the book, *Faces of Suicide, Volume 1,"* available on Amazon as a Kindle book. She has also been a guest on Grief Diaries

Radio twice in 2014, both episodes are available on iTunes. At the time of this publication she is working on a new book called, *Advice from Tomorrow*.

*

ERICA BELTZ
Erica's 5-year-old son Luke Jordan died in 2002
from a fallen banister in his aunt's driveway
lukeslove5@gmail.com

Erica Gale Beltz was born in Herrin, Illinois, the youngest of three. The family moved frequently, finally settling in western Georgia when Erica was eight. At eighteen, Erica gave birth to her daughter, Lakin, who was born fighting for her life. Five years later, Erica gave birth to Luke.

Struggling with alcoholism, drug abuse and domestic violence, Erica worked backwards to find her footing. Erica has been a general manager at J. Christopher's in Marietta, Georgia, for the past three years, and been with the company for eight. Despite her daughter's serious medical needs, Erica has volunteered extensively for The Compassionate Friends, including serving as group leader, co-leader, facilitator instructor and event coordinator. She also volunteers for Kate's Club, a club for grieving children. Erica is co-author of *Grief*

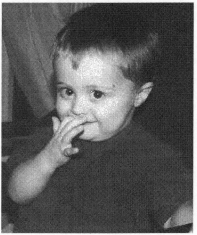

Diaries: Surviving Loss of a Child . Her first grandchild, Ava Kate, was due on Luke's Angel Day, and has brought a joy into Erica's life that keeps her heart singing. She and her fiancé just bought a home where they reside with their English bulldog MollyGirl.

*

SOPHIE BLOWERS
Sophie was 50 when her mother Amy
died at age 79 of internal bleeding
SophieBlowers1@gmail.com

Stephanie Blowers was born in North Virginia in the mid 1960s. She was a stay-at-home mom, raising and home educating her four children for twenty-five years. Once her youngest graduated from high school, Stephanie returned to school herself, and earned a degree in paralegal studies. Stephanie now works for a pro bono law firm. Stephanie's true passion is in the support of the newly bereaved, using her heightened empathy skills to create a safe place for the griever as the overwhelming reality of loss is realized.

*

LYNDA CHELDELIN FELL
Lynda's 15-year-old daughter Aly
died in a car accident in 2009
www.lyndafell.com * lynda@lyndafell.com

Born and raised in the Pacific Northwest, Lynda Cheldelin Fell is a mother and grandmother who treasures moments of joy, laughter, and the little things in life. In 2009, Lynda and her beloved husband lost their third child, a fifteen-year-old competitive swimmer named Aly, in a tragic car accident while coming home from watching the U.S. Open in Seattle. Surrounded by love and support, Lynda was determined to overcome the darkness and was just finding her

footing when her forty-six-year-old husband suffered a major stroke leaving him with permanent disabilities. Seeing the world through the filter of sorrow, Lynda found comfort by helping others who were struggling, and this fueled her passion to create a legacy of help, healing and hope through storytelling.

*

MICHELLE DETWILER
Michelle's 19-year-old daughter Emily
died in 2014 due to congenital complications
mdetwiler@yahoo.com

Michelle Detwiler and her husband, Jeff, have raised four children in Washington state. Former foster parents for seventeen years, they adopted two of their four children through the state. Michelle's career experiences have been varied.

Aside from foster care, she was also at one time a medical assistant, an electronics technician, and a regular contributing writer for *Preemie* magazine.

Michelle owns an embroidery business, and works as a professional embroiderer. She also loves all kinds of crafts, especially making mini scrapbooks.

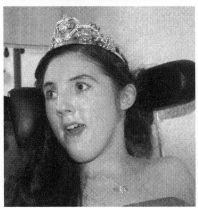

*
CHRISTINE DUMINIAK
Christine's 86 year-old mother Ann
died from an abdominal aortic aneurysm in 2004
www.ChristineDuminiak.com * ChrisDuminiak@aol.com

Christine Duminiak is a Certified Grief Recovery Specialist, radio host, author, speaker, and founder of Prayer Wave for After-Death Communications.

Duminiak has been a guest on many TV and radio shows, including Fox & Friends, Good Day Philadelphia, The God Squad, the Arizona Midday Show, NBC, CBS, and Coast-to-Coast AM and is a frequent keynote speaker at grief seminars.

Christine is the author of *Heaven Talks to Children*, *After-Death Communication: God's Gift of Love*, and two children's books, *Grammy Visits From Heaven* and *Grandpa Visits From Heaven*.

*

SHARON EHLERS
Sharon's best friend Joy died in 2009 at age 52
Sharon's former fiancé John died in 2012 at age 59
sharon@grief-reiki.com * www.grief-reiki.com

Sharon (Skura) Ehlers was born and raised in Los Angeles, California. She is most passionate about her three beautiful children, ages thirty-three, twenty-three and twenty-one. She has loving parents and a beautiful sister who also live in Los Angeles.

After the suicides of a close friend and a former fiancé within a two-year period, Sharon was confused about how many people either avoided her or didn't want to talk about these events. In her grief, she tried to make sense of it all, but it seemed like it was "never the right time" to bring it up with anyone. So Sharon took a deep breath and tried to work through the grief on her own. Her thought was that there had to be a better way. So after working in corporate America for almost thirty years, Sharon started her own company, Grief Reiki® LLC, to offer a multidimensional approach to grief through emotional recovery and spiritual healing. Now a certified grief recovery specialist® and award-winning author of *Grief Diaries: Surviving Loss by Suicide*, Sharon is helping others heal and recover from grief by providing them with a safe, compassionate and healing environment for their journey. Her best lesson in life is: "Miracles do happen."

*
ANNAH ELIZABETH
Annah's son Gavin Michael aspirated on his meconium
during the delivery and died 26 minutes following his birth
www.TheFiveFacets.com * thefivefacets@aol.com

Annah Elizabeth is an author, speaker, and the creator of The Five Facets Philosophy on Healing™, a groundbreaking guide that helps others live their best personal, professional and philanthropic lives in the face of adversity. She authored the book *Digging for the Light* and coauthored *Grief Diaries: Surviving Loss of a Child* and *Grief Diaries: How to Help the Newly Bereaved*.

Motivated by personal tragedy including the death of her firstborn, miscarriage, infidelity and severe depression, Annah Elizabeth set out to uncover the secrets that

allow people to triumph over tragedy. Through her explorations of loss, grief and healing, Annah not only discovered that the answers are as universal as the mystery itself, but also unearthed essential grief event recovery tools which she assembled into an innovative program, one that teaches us how to solve grief puzzles by identifying, evaluating, and refashioning conflicts with intent and purpose. Annah's work pioneers a new discussion, and provides the roadmap that helps us make the transition from grief to healing. Born and raised in North Carolina, Annah lives in upstate New York with her husband and numerous pets, in a soon-to-be empty nest, but that is just geography. Annah feels at home wherever her life and work lead her. Got Grief? Get Healing.™ with Annah Elizabeth and The Five Facets.

*
DAPHNE GREER
Daphne's 5-year-old daughter Lydia died in 2008 in a
car accident during a routine morning commute
www.grievinggumdrops.com

Daphne Greer is a native of eastern Oregon, where she resides with her husband, Jake, and their four living children where she enjoys the country lifestyle and love for the outdoors. She spent thirteen years as an adult parole officer.

Following the tragic death of her daughter in 2008, Daphne found a new purpose and passion in life. She co-founded a nonprofit in memory of her daughter Lydia which provides birthday celebrations to children in need. She also blogs about finding hope amid grief and loss. She is a member of the Oregon Christian Writers Association, and also served for five years on the steering committee of The Compassionate Friends in Salem, Oregon. She

volunteers with Ellie's Way, a nonprofit organization that provides outreach for the bereaved.

Daphne coauthored *Grief Diaries: Will We Survive?* and has contributed to *Miracles and Moments of Grace, Inspiring Stories of Survival*, and *The Mom Quilt*. Daphne's memoir in progress was a finalist in the Cascade Writing Contest in 2015.

*
BRENDA L. KLEINSASSER
Brenda's 88 year-old mother died
from congestive heart failure in 2011
brendasbrainstorm.blogspot.com

Brenda Kleinsasser resides in Bismarck, North Dakota, the capital city. Brenda has worked in various avenues of the medical field for over thirty years. Brenda served as editor of the CreakyJoints Poet's Corner (& Artists too), for three years, a unique online publication where the emphasis is on encouraging those who live with a chronic illness to allow their creativity to shine.

Brenda is also a fierce patient advocate for both brain tumors and rheumatoid arthritis, as she has also lived with RA for over twenty-four years. Her stance on advocacy is speaking up for those who cannot, or feel they have no voice. Brenda has testified to that end in her own state of North Dakota, representing the patient's voice on behalf of the Global Healthy Living Foundation, via the 50 State Network as a super advocate. Brenda is also a volunteer for Patient Partners in Research with CreakyJoints. In her spare time she enjoys writing her blog, Brenda's Brainstorm and Trevor, a golden retriever who is her storyteller and helper with spreading awareness and hope. Brenda also enjoys journaling, singing and reading.

Brenda coauthored *Real Life Diaries: Living with a Brain Injury* and *Real Life Diaries: Living with Rheumatoid Disease*, and contributed to *Grief Diaries: Loss of Health*.

*
DEANA MARTIN
Deana's only two children, 25-year-old Amanda
and 21-year-old Logan, died in a car accident in 2011
www.CryForMeNoMore.com * deana@cryformenomore.com

Deana Martin is a childless parent, who lost her only two children in a tragic auto accident in 2011. A third young man, Deana's future son-in-law, was also killed in the car. Miraculously, Deana was spared her only grand-daughter who was in the car behind them. Since the death of her children Deana has become a certified grief specialist, and has channeled the love for her children to other families facing loss. Before this life-changing tragedy, Deana was a project manager in the pharmaceutical industry, and had enjoyed a twenty-five-year career with several Fortune 500 pharmaceutical companies, starting with Eli Lilly in 1988, the year her son was born.

She is vice president of Cry For Me, No More, coauthor of *Grief Diaries: Surviving Loss of a Child,* has contributed to a number of titles in the Grief Diaries series, and serves on the board of the National Grief & Hope Coalition. She has faced many adversities in life and feels each one makes her stronger. She is a breast cancer survivor, and is no stranger to trauma. She hopes to help people heal by showing them how to find the strength and courage needed along the journey.

*
DIANE MCKENZIE-SAPP
Diane's 65-year-old husband Ron died from renal failure in 2006
widowsring@gmail.com * www.ExpressionOfGrief.com

Diane McKenzie-Sapp, a Maryland native, has been an airline stewardess, dental assistant, department store manager and buyer, and has been a hospice nurse, an assistant director of Nursing and an inspector for Medicare. She can handcraft Christmas ornaments, crochet, quilt, paint ceramic nativity sets, canvas, wood, glass and mailboxes, and she trained for ten years to teach and make porcelain dolls. She reads medical and herbal texts for fun. Ron and Diane's village included three children, a family of parents, siblings, friends and pets. Asked why she could not settle on one career, she cited Matthew parable 25:14-30 "Talents" and the consequences of neglecting a God-given talent. She broke tradition by

crafting new unconventional solutions. Seeing an unattractive photo of an open-mouthed tearful girl, she stopped crying at age four. At age six she decided being ticklish was a weakness. She was relentless until her "why nots" were answered. All suffer a broken heart with grief. Finding a way to heal that heart, the child became stronger than the widow. That unwavering determination for solutions to problems by challenging with "Why Not?" led to unconventional ways to view grief and offer widow's rings to the world.

*

JULIE MJELVE
Julie's 42-year-old husband Cameron died by suicide in 2011
www.grievingtogether.ca * julie@grievingtogether.ca

Julie (McCargar) Mjelve was born in Edmonton, Alberta, Canada.
She completed her BSC in Physical Therapy in 1992. After working
as a physical therapist for ten years, Julie spent almost eight months
traveling Europe before returning to Edmonton to complete her
master's in Education, specializing in teaching English as a second
language. In 2007 Julie married James Cameron Mjelve. Julie and
Cameron went on to have three beautiful children, one boy and two
girls. As the demands of child raising increased, Julie's work shifted
from teaching English as a second language to internationally
educated nurses to working as an academic strategist with a local
college. Following the birth of their second child, Julie became a
stay-at-home mom, focusing on the care and attention her children
required. Currently, Julie has started her own business, along with
two other partners, called Grieving Together which provides
mourning symbols to those who are grieving.

*
MARY POTTER KENYON
Mary's 60-year-old husband David died of heart failure in 2012
marypotterkenyon@gmail.com * www.marypotterkenyon.com

Mary Potter Kenyon graduated from the University of Northern Iowa and is a reporter for the Manchester Press newspaper in Iowa. She is a widely published author, workshop presenter and sought-after public speaker.

Mary has contributed to a number of titles in the Grief Diaries series, and coauthored *Grief Diaries: Poetry & Prose and More.*

Familius has published four of her books including *Coupon Crazy: The Science, the Savings and the Stories Behind America's Extreme Obsession, Chemo-Therapist: How Cancer Cured a Marriage, Refined By Fire: A Journey of Grief and Grace,* and she coauthored *Mary & Me: A Lasting Link Through Ink.*

Several of Mary's devotions were published in Zondervan's *Hope in the Mourning* Bible and an essay about the connection between grief and creativity was published in the January/February issue of *Poets & Writers* magazine. Mary lives in Iowa with two of her eight children.

*

NANCY REDMOND
Nancy's 40-year-old husband Kevin
died of a heart attack in 2012

Nancy Jeannine Redmond was born and raised in St. Paul, Minnesota, and has lived in the Oakdale area (a suburb of St. Paul) for the past thirty-two years. She is the mother of three wonderful children, thirty year-old Ryan, twenty-seven year-old Christopher and twenty-three year-old Rachel. She is also "Grammy" to the littlest love of her life, seven year-old Jayden Ryan, and a new grandchild expected early fall 2016. She shares her home with three beautiful kitties, Maxx, Makale'a and Maggie, as well as a Shih Tzu/Pekingese furry love (Chloe) and a three-pound Teacup Yorkie (Rusty). Nancy is, by profession, a medical transcriptionist, secretary and coder, and has specialized in the fields of OB-GYN, ophthalmology, orthopedics and most recently, pathology. Her  hobbies including agate and rock hunting on the shores of beautiful Lake Superior. Her most beloved hobby is taking amazing photos of flowers, her grandson and the magic of raindrops. Many summer mornings, before the dew has dried, you'll find her in her pajamas and barefoot in her garden catching the glorious sunrise shining on dew drops! She also designs and creates essential oil diffusing jewelry, and is particularly drawn to creating jewelry with Mookaite (Australian) jasper.

*

MARYELLEN ROACH
MaryEllen's sister, Suzette and two nieces, 6-year-old
Vivian and 8-year-old Lillian, died in car accident in 2012

MaryEllen Roach was raised on a forty-acre farm in southern Illinois where her family raised sheep and other animals. MaryEllen graduated high school in 1996 with honors. She moved to St. Louis, Missouri, at the age of nineteen, where she modeled, and also worked for large companies based in St. Louis. After the loss of her older sister and two young nieces, MaryEllen, her parents Marvin and Yvonna, her younger sister, Ashley and Ashley's husband, Moi, all moved to northern California, where they currently reside.

*

MARY LEE ROBINSON
Mary Lee's 63-year-old husband Pat
died from a sudden stroke in 2013
www.MaryLeeRobinson.com * mary-lee-robinson.myshopify.com

Mary Lee Robinson is a native of Towson, Maryland, and has lived in Maryland, Pennsylvania, and West Virginia. She now resides in South Carolina, where she retired (she thought) with her husband shortly before his death.

Mary Lee authored *The Widow or Widower Next Door,* coauthor of *Grief Diaries: Surviving Loss of a Spouse,* and *Grief Diaries: How to Help the Newly Bereaved,* and the owner of Rings of Remembrance.

A member of American Association of Christian Counselors, Mary Lee is a certified grief coach and also organizes social clubs for widows and widowers.

*

ALEXIS VON UTTER
Alexis was 12 when her father, Marc,
died at age 57 from lung cancer complications

Alexis Von Utter was born in Boynton Beach, Florida. She moved with her family at age three to Maryland. She attended St. Andrew Apostle School from kindergarten until fifth grade, St. Bernadette's School from sixth to eighth grade, Bishop O'Connell High School for her freshman year, and now attends the Academy of the Holy Cross. Alexis loves to play soccer,

basketball and softball, and she plays competitive softball in high school. She is very fun-loving, enjoys people and loves to help out.

Alexis works at a mall near her home, and loves the interaction she has daily at the register. She loves to tell her story to help others, and finds it interesting how many she can heal with it.

*

HEATHER WALLACE-REY
Heather was 40 when her father, John,
died suddenly at age 71 of a massive heart attack
www.fivegallonsofcrazy.com * heathercatherine0702@gmail.com

Heather was raised in the suburbs of Chicago, and attended Coe College in Cedar Rapids, Iowa. She has been active in ministry for eighteen years in youth ministries, and has led workshops that benefit youth and Christian educators. Heather serves on the Annual Events Committee for The Association of Presbyterian Church Educators, has had opportunities to speak at Faith & Grief events (www.faithandgrief.org).

Heather and her husband, David, are the parents of the five most wonderful young people in the universe: Ryan, Gordon, Hannah, Nate and Jack, who make her laugh until she cries, daily. Heather enjoys blogging, gardening, public speaking, and spending time with friends and family. Heather's goals in life include being remembered by her family, finding time to vacuum while singing show tunes, being the personal assistant of her favorite children's author (www.gotyourcape.com), and having the opportunity to perform a monologue on the porch of her childhood friend, somewhere in North Carolina, while he pretends not to know her.

Heather authored *Faith, Grief and Pass The Chocolate Pudding*, and coauthored *Grief Diaries: Surviving Loss of a Parent*.

*
DIANNE WEST
Dianne's 69-year-old husband, Vern, died from multiple myeloma in 2010
www.soaringspirits.org * bravegirlsclub.com
amyelomawidowsjourney.blogspot.com dianneinnv@gmail.com

Originally from a small town in southeast Michigan, Dianne married at eighteen, and was blessed to share forty-one years with her husband, Vern. She was his caregiver for over four years as he fought multiple myeloma, a blood cancer that attacks the bone marrow. Widowed in 2010, Dianne has dedicated her post-loss life to giving back to the widowed community. In 2013, she was asked to become the National Volunteer Coordinator for Soaring Spirits International, a nonprofit that serves to provide resources and peer support to people who have lost a spouse or life partner. She serves as the administrator of Widowed Village and coordinates volunteers for Camp Widow in Tampa, San Diego and Toronto. Additionally, she oversees the

Soaring Spirits Regional Group program, local communities of widowed friends throughout North America, and co-leads a group in the Las Vegas area. Dianne retired from the Las Vegas Valley Water District in 2015 after twenty-nine years of service, and has joined the Brave Girl University teaching team as a mentor for widows.

THANK YOU

I am deeply indebted to the writers who contributed to *Grief Diaries: How to Help the Newly Bereaved*. It required tremendous courage to relive such painful moments for the purpose of helping others, and the collective dedication to seeing this project to the end is a legacy to be proud of. Special thanks to author Annah Elizabeth and award-winning writer Emily Barnhardt for the use of their submissions that were relocated in part and used to craft many of the chapter introductions. I'm also grateful to our Grief Diaries village and the lovely souls I consider dear friends, collaborative partners, mentors, and muses. I treasure each and every one of you!

Helen Keller once said, "Walking with a friend in the dark is better than walking alone in the light. By sharing our struggles, we learn that we aren't truly alone as we travel our journey, for there are others ahead of us and some behind us. That is what Grief Diaries is all about.

CREATOR, Grief Diaries

Shared joy is double joy.
Shared sorrow is half a sorrow.
SWEDISH PROVERB

CREDITS

During extensive editing of this book's first edition some excerpts, expressions, and phrases were removed from contributing author's submissions and subsequently placed elsewhere in the text. This credit page identifies some of those materials, but please note that any and all affected content remains under the copyright protection of the original author, which may be different than what is printed.

Emily Barnhardt's excerpt submissions and contributions, as originally submitted:

- "In most cases, people say statements like these with purely good intentions, and it's important to note that. However, hurtful words can still resonate deeply in the fragile heart of someone grieving, so it's beneficial for support people to do their best to think about what they're going to say before they say it.

- "I don't think we ever truly intend to minimize someone else's suffering. I think it happens because it's so easy for us, when we are on the outside of someone else's sorrow and grief, to see a picture in our minds of what healing will look like and how that person should go about finding it. We want desperately to help that person move from sorrow into victory as fast as possible. And that very immense desire and love to help a grieving person could actually rob us, at times, of our God-given need for simple moments of human relationship and intimacy." –*What Not to Say*, pg. 24

- "Truthfully, no words are even necessary in those moments – just a comforting, loving presence can bring so much comfort and warmth in the harsh and cold experience of loss. We often think it's our words that make a difference, but it's not. It's our love and our heart and our willingness to be available." –*What Not to Say*, pg. 24 (originally submitted for *What to Do*)

- Illustration credit to Emily for the "I'm Fine" artwork in *What Not to Say*, pg. 30

Annah Elizabeth's excerpt submissions and contributions, as originally submitted:

- "Sometimes we avoid reaching out because we are afraid to say or do the wrong thing, especially since what is so right for one person can be so wrong for another. For most people who are suffering, silence is one of our worst fears. Silence has a way of validating our skewed thinking that what we are experiencing isn't really real, it validates our worries that our feelings and thoughts aren't rational, and it sends the message that we should "be over it" by now.

  "Though these signals are seldom intended, that is often how they are perceived. The other important note is that quite often the bereaved just need someone to vent to, someone with whom they can share, someone to simply do nothing more than listen as they release the heartbreak from their soul. Bottling our fears creates toxins that exacerbate our suffering, whereas spilling our sadness helps to make room for healing." ~*What Not to Say*

- "In times of significant loss or deep grief, words are inadequate to describe how we, ourselves, are feeling and are equally unable to express our empathy for another. Adding to this dilemma is the simple truth that what might be so completely right for one person might be so totally wrong for another.
  "So what are we to do? The best thing we can do is follow our heart, to summon the strength that sits in our gut, to recall the words that have been helpful to us and then to share. The best we have to offer is the best of ourselves, which is nothing more than love. Share your love in whatever capacity you are able to share." ~*What Not to Say* (originally submitted to *What to Say*)

- "There are so many, many opportunities to help someone in their time of need and the only limitation is your imagination. One of the key things to remember is to offer only the help you can provide, for when someone accepts help, they are often relying on and looking forward to whatever assistance you have offered. Look into your heart and your day planner and your cupboards to discover what help you are able to offer. I often say that you can tell how much a person enjoys the work they are doing because it shows in every little detail. No matter how small you perceive an act of kindness to be, chances are it will ripple through the receiver for years to come." ~*What to Do*

- "One of the most important things to remember is to offer only the help you can comfortably provide. People who are grieving, especially in the early days and months often don't know what they need or want and thus find it difficult to answer the question "What do you need/can we do?" When we offer assistance that works for us, our means, and our schedules, we are less likely to run into problems. When our support is accepted, the bereaved person often looks forward to and/or is depending on that help, and when it falls through or doesn't materialize it then creates more stress, which is something none of us wants to do." ~*More Ways to Help*

- "*Let me count the ways I will respond to you*, whisper the bereaved. If we could paint our sense, sensibilities, and sensitivities onto a mural, it would look a bit like one enormous, circular scribble. Scrawl after scrawl, in red and orange and yellow and pink and purple and black and blue.

  "Sometimes we are able to temper our emotions and sometimes they come spewing from us like vomit. It's not right. It's not wrong. Sometimes it's not fair. It is sorrow, both measured and unmeasured." ~*Understanding our Reactions*

- "Change. Change often positions us in places where we feel inadequate, isolated, and unprepared. Change sometimes feels as if we have embarked on a journey with no companion, no compass, and no light.

  "And yet, our pack is never empty. The bag's fibers are woven with memory and love and it is filled with the many tokens and tools we collected on earlier travels. Those are the things that keep us company, guide us, and illuminate our way.

  "You, Journeyer, are a big part of our survival pack. Never doubt it for a second." ~Understanding our Comfort (originally submitted for Understanding our Needs)

- "Every journey is unique for we carry in our backpacks different experiences, different beliefs, different desires, different needs, different tolerances and we walk different roads. Though we may not see anyone else on the path we trod, we are never truly alone for more walking wounded move behind, beside, and in front of us. We are students and teachers alike. We borrow one another's books on life, loss, and living and we weave fragments of their travel stories and their successes into our own." ~*What We Want You to Know* (originally submitted to *Understanding our Journey*)

*

ABOUT

LYNDA CHELDELIN FELL

Considered a pioneer in the field of inspirational hope in the aftermath of hardship and loss, Lynda Cheldelin Fell has a passion for storytelling and producing groundbreaking projects that create a legacy of help, healing, and hope.

She is the creator of the 5-star book series *Grief Diaries* and *Real Life Diaries*, and CEO of AlyBlue Media. Her repertoire of interviews include Dr. Martin Luther King's daughter, Trayvon Martin's mother, sisters of the late Nicole Brown Simpson, Pastor Todd Burpo of Heaven Is For Real, CNN commentator Dr. Ken Druck, and other societal newsmakers on finding healing and hope in the aftermath of life's harshest challenges.

Lynda's own story began in 2007, when she had an alarming dream about her young teenage daughter, Aly. In the dream, Aly was a backseat passenger in a car that veered off the road and sailed into a lake. Aly sank with the car, leaving behind an open book floating face down on the water. Two years later, Lynda's dream became reality when her daughter was killed as a backseat passenger in a car accident while coming home from a swim meet. Overcome with grief, Lynda's forty-six-year-old husband suffered a major stroke that left him with severe disabilities, changing the family dynamics once again.

The following year, Lynda was invited to share her remarkable story about finding hope after loss, and she accepted. That cathartic experience inspired her to create groundbreaking projects spanning national events, radio, film and books to help others who share the same journey feel less alone. Now considered one of the foremost grief educators and healing facilitators in the United States, Lynda is dedicated to helping ordinary people share their own stories of survival and hope in the aftermath of loss.

lynda@lyndafell.com | www.lyndafell.com | www.griefdiaries.com

ALYBLUE MEDIA TITLES

Grief Diaries: Impact Statement
Grief Diaries: Hit by Impaired Driver
Grief Diaries: Surviving Loss of a Spouse
Grief Diaries: Surviving Loss of a Child
Grief Diaries: Surviving Loss of a Sibling
Grief Diaries: Surviving Loss of a Parent
Grief Diaries: Surviving Loss of an Infant
Grief Diaries: Surviving Loss of a Loved One
Grief Diaries: Surviving Loss by Suicide
Grief Diaries: Surviving Loss of Health
Grief Diaries: How to Help the Newly Bereaved
Grief Diaries: Loss by Impaired Driving
Grief Diaries: Loss by Homicide
Grief Diaries: Loss of a Pregnancy
Grief Diaries: Hello from Heaven
Grief Diaries: Grieving for the Living
Grief Diaries: Shattered
Grief Diaries: Project Cold Case
Grief Diaries: Poetry & Prose and More
Grief Diaries: Through the Eyes of Men
Grief Diaries: Will We Survive?
Real Life Diaries: Living with a Brain Injury
Real Life Diaries: Through the Eyes of DID
Real Life Diaries: Through the Eyes of an Eating Disorder
Real Life Diaries: Living with Mental Illness
Real Life Diaries: Living with Gastroparesis
Real Life Diaries: Living with Endometriosis
Grammy Visits From Heaven
Grandpa Visits From Heaven
Faith, Grief & Pass the Chocolate Pudding
Heaven Talks to Children
Color My Soul Whole
Grief Reiki

Humanity's legacy of stories and storytelling
is the most precious we have.

DORIS LESSING

*

To share your story, visit
www.griefdiaries.com
www.RealLifeDiaries.com

PUBLISHED BY ALYBLUE MEDIA
Inside every human is a story worth sharing.
www.AlyBlueMedia.com

Made in the USA
Columbia, SC
04 December 2021

50100667R00176